# COMMUNICATING WITH A FORMER SPOUSE

# *COMMUNICATING WITH A FORMER SPOUSE*

*Thoughts and Experiences for
Greater Relationships
and a Happier Life
for Our Children*

Vincent Gerard Molina

**Signature Publishing**

Copyright © 1999 by Vincent Gerard Molina

All rights reserved. Printed in the United States of America. No part of this publication may be reproduced, stored in a retrieval system or transmitted in any form or electronic, mechanical, photocopy, recording or otherwise, without written permission of the publisher, except in the case of brief quotations embodied in critical articles and reviews.

FIRST EDITION

Edited by Lee Ann Rotzien
Cover Design by Alison Brush and Perry Van Schelt

Library of Congress Catalog Number: 97-91900
ISBN 0-9657536-0-3

Signature Publishing, 2335 S. West Temple, Salt Lake City, UT 84115

I would like to thank and acknowledge the people that have been quoted in this book for adding to the message we have worked on delivering to our readers. It has been our intent to maintain accuracy and obtain all necessary permissions to reprint material and use quotes. We apologize for any errors and are willing to provide a correction in future editions.

Definitions used in the beginning of some chapters were extracted from the *American Heritage Dictionary,* based on the new Second College Edition, 1983 and the *Random House Dictionary of the English Language,* Second Edition Unabridged, 1987.

We would like to acknowledge the following publishers and individuals for permission to reprint the following material:

Beetle Bailey cartoon by Mort Walker ©1995, King Features Syndicate. Reprinted by permission of King Features Syndicate. All rights reserved.

The Buckets cartoon ©1995, Tribune Media Services. Reprinted by permission of United Features Syndicate. All rights reserved.

Dave cartoons by Dave Miller ©1995 and 1997, Tribune Media Services. Reprinted by permission of Tribune Media Services. All rights reserved.

Non Sequitur cartoon ©1995, Washington Post Writers Group. Reprinted by permission of The Washington Post. All rights reserved.

Ziggy cartoon by Tom Wilson ©1995, Universal Press Syndicate. Reprinted by permission of Universal Press Syndicate. All rights reserved.

*This book is to be read over and over again.*

# Dedication

*Communicating with a Former Spouse* is written for all the children who have experienced the divorce of their parents, who number approximately one million each year. It is the author's belief that through improved communication between former spouses, children will experience a greater degree of happiness. Children are our hope for the future. They deserve to be in an environment that promotes unconditional love and cooperation between their parents. Adults are the example. What we show our children has a direct impact on their self-esteem and view of the world. Show them love and they will learn to love. Show them hate and they will learn to hate. Communicating with a former spouse is only one aspect of our ability to communicate. How we communicate with our children both verbally and non-verbally will be reflected in their performance in school, home, by their actions in social settings as well as their own personal relations and choices.

Parents need to take responsibility for the words they use. They not only need to; they have to. It doesn't matter whether the choice to bring a child into this world was planned or unplanned, it is the parents' responsibility to provide an atmosphere conducive to the children's well being. Children do not come with instruction manuals. If being a responsible parent means seeking professional advice, then do it. It if means attending parenting classes, then do it. If it means learning new communicating techniques, skill or ideas then do it. Whatever it takes during a marriage, or in the aftermath of divorce, it is never too late.

*Communicating with a Former Spouse* was originally conceived with the simple yet profoundly important thought that former spouses deserved to have greater relationships and happier lives. If communication were to increase from the extreme of nonexistence to even the most minimal level, it would constitute a success. Any level of improved communication is a blessing. A price cannot be placed on improved communication with a former spouse, which creates not only better relationships and a happier life for themselves, but also benefits the children.

It is further the belief of the author that all the time, energy and money spent on counseling for the children could be significantly reduced if the parents would only learn to create "functional" communication within their relationship. If you have a child with another person with whom you must communicate, you are in a relationship. This relationship can be experienced with dignity and unconditional love.

So, to all the children of divorced families, *Communicating with a Former Spouse* is offered as a stepping stone that brings you closer to having more love in your lives.

# Acknowledgments

This is a work of love and many have to be thanked for their influence, participation, and support, for without them I would not had the inspiration and drive to complete it. The amount of those who supported this project would be a book in itself.

I am grateful to the following people:

Melanie, my wife, who came into my life at a time that brought clarity to this project and has been the most supportive partner that anyone could want.

Hollie and Shayna, my daughters, who give me their unconditional love, they are two of God's angels that were sent to teach me lessons that only they could deliver.

*Vincent Gerard Molina*

Gerard and Violet Molina, my parents, who provided a household full of love and allowing me to grow even when it was more painful for them. Lee Ann, my sister, who has been one of my closest confidants over the years, and whose guidance has benefited me greatly. David, my brother, who allows me to love him enough to trust my words and support him. Rose Helen Vincent, my aunt, who taught me to strive and do the best I could.

To the mothers of my daughters, they have remained open to working with me in the raising of two beautiful girls.

David Rose, a trusted friend and consultant, who guided me through this journey. James Burk, a remarkable human being and attorney, who has a heart of gold. Barry Spilchuk, an advisor, who provided focus, viable solutions, and much needed, hugs. Jack Canfield and Mark Victor Hansen, their love to teach and mentor through different forums and venues, answers questions and give direction openly that have been vital to my work. Eve Hogan, whose friendship and support contributed to knowing that I would succeed.

Cloudsifter Flood, who performed the first edit of this book and made me laugh as we deciphered my notes. Gaile Sickel, who provided constant support while I traveled highs and lows, challenges, and opportunities. Sharan Ro, who has a special gift, the ability to help others and facilitate positive change. Tara Chappell, who provided valuable input and helped to make this project the best it can be.

Gerald DeCorte and Alfred Orta, two of my long time friends, we have grown and learned many lessons together over the past twenty years. Fred Delong, who years ago saw my potential, and invested his time and energy to groom me for the corporate world that led to many of my life successes. Herbert K. Horita, a visionary and a mentor, took the time to share his wisdom with me.

Sheri Nievaard, a dedicated assistant, has been a valuable asset to the company and this project. Paul and Nancy Clemens at Blue Dolphin Publishing, Inc., both radiate love and support to everyone, and offer opportunity to so many people who have a message that must be heard by others. Berny, Lynn, and Tony Dohrmann, respected and loved supporters, of Income Builders International (IBI) Free Enterprise Forum, where dreams can and do come true. Without them, and the literally thousands of friends and contacts I have had the honor of meeting in the past few years, people like myself would not have an opportunity to live their dream.

And, to the many people who have supported my endeavors, you too are important, without you this book would not have been possible. Know that I love you for being a part of this gift to families.

# Contents

| | |
|---|---|
| Foreword | xix |
| Preface | xxiii |
| About the Title | xxvii |
| The Beginning | 1 |
| Chapter I - Divorce: More Difficult Than Marriage? | 9 |
|    *A Common Communication Blunder* | *12* |
|    *Trust* | *15* |
|    *Overcoming Expectations And Patterns* | *19* |

## Chapter II - Goals After Marriage     33

*Setting Goals and Moving into Action*     37
*Stretching Our Comfort Zone*     39
*"Love Means Never Having to . . ."*     41
*Changing Our Communication Diet*     43
*Red Ants*     45
*Criminals of Marriage*     50
*Forgiveness*     53

## Chapter III - You See Me but Do You Hear Me?     65

*Listening . . . a Lost Art*     72
*There Is More Than One Road to Travel*     76
*Setting Boundaries for Manageable Change*     82
*Unexpected Challenges and Payoffs*     92

## Chapter IV - Support:
Emotional, Physical, Financial & Spiritual     97

*Emotional Support*     104
*Physical Support*     107
*Financial Support*     111
*Spiritual Support*     116

## Chapter V - Your Personal Life, My Personal Life:
What Is Off Limits?     121

## Chapter VI - "What Works and What Doesn't?" 133

*A Note on Avoidance* 146
*Children* 148
*Now It Is Your Turn . . .* 153

## Chapter VII - Happily Ever After: Can It Happen? 161

*Choices in Life* 164
*Desire and . . .* 168
*New Relationships* 175
*The Real Victims* 177
*Abundance* 181
*It Can Happen* 184

# Foreword

You are about to embark on a journey. This journey may take you over a few bumpy trails, but I guarantee you that the final destination will be well worth your effort. The goal for this trip is a return to love, understanding, and respect.

Right from the opening pages, this book will allow you to reclaim your dignity and work towards mutual respect. You will learn why "former spouse" is so much more empowering than "ex". You will learn about setting boundaries on your new personal lives now that you are apart, and you will learn how to deal with the children in a loving, nurturing manner.

There are many reasons why I agreed to write the foreword to this book. Here are a few of the main ones:

1) Vincent Molina is a good man! He is a loving, concerned person who genuinely cares about others.

2) The principles work! If you put to use the ideas in this book with clear intent, you will lift all your relationships to a higher level.

3) If you have children, they will become the beneficiaries of all of your efforts. They are worth it, and so are you.

This book is not designed to reunite you with your former spouse. However, we know of people who were about to be separated or divorced, who have used the communication principles contained in these pages, and ultimately reconciled. It is rather ironic. If the people needing this book now could have had access to these communication principles during their marriage, many would still be part of a united couple.

Vincent Molina has, through experience, created a communication handbook that will afford former couples many benefits: the regaining of their personal power, enhancement of their self-esteem, and the opportunity to communicate with dignity and respect. What I feel is most important, if there are children involved, is that the parents get to demonstrate to their children what mature, caring adults act like when they want to be responsible role models. Another great benefit for the children is that they realize that their parents' breakup was not their fault!

I am a personal development trainer and the main topics of my workshops include: developing self-esteem, letting go of the past, and relationship enhancement. I have also had the privilege of co-authoring one of the books in the internationally best selling series, *Chicken Soup for the Soul*. My book, *A Cup of Chicken Soup for the Soul*, has served over a half of a million people. The series, as a whole, has helped millions of people around the world. My life's purpose, and the main focus of the *Chicken Soup* books, is to show people how to have more love and understanding in their lives. *Communicating With A Former Spouse* ties into the same mission perfectly.

I am not a professional counselor, nor have I been divorced. But the very nature of my work has put me into a counseling role. In this role, many times I have been exposed to individuals and couples who need communication and coping strategies to deal with their break-ups. (Coincidentally, I am writing this forward while on a five-hour plane flight. When my seat-mate saw the title of this book she immediately remarked, "Boy, is that book ever needed!")

I think the ultimate testimonial for this book was given even before Vincent finished writing the words.

*Vincent Gerard Molina*

When Vincent's former spouse (Shayna's mother) heard that he was writing the book she immediately sat down and wrote a testimonial letter stating that Vincent, by virtue of the growth he has gone through, has every right to author this book. She should know. She has lived and grown through the process as well.

Her letter brought tears to my eyes, and I immediately asked Vincent if I could read the manuscript. Well I have read it, and you are about to. Enjoy the ride because the road to love, understanding, and respect is a fun and worthwhile trip!

With love and respect,

Barry Spilchuk, co-author,
*A Cup of Chicken Soup for the Soul*

# Preface

*Communicating with a Former Spouse* is a book for those who want to improve communication. It is a book that assists people with communicating skills. It is for those who are looking for practical communication tips. These tips were derived from individuals who have shared their situations and are delivered through the author's own paralleled experiences.

This book is written primarily in the first person to relate to the reader that they are not alone and what is occurring in their life is not exclusive to them. Although there are many other situations that may not be covered in this book, *Communicating with a Former Spouse* was written to keep the information imparted to its simplest form without delving into the clinical realm.

*Communicating with a Former Spouse* is not meant to replace nor act as a counseling tool, but shares skills and situations to be contemplated, applied, and used in conjunction with any formal counseling that one may have benefited from or is receiving. This information can be used on its own and is successful because it coaches communication skills and language, *not* therapy. This book was written to help and serve those who want to improve their overall situation for the benefit of the children, as well as themselves, in an area of communication where help is not offered on a broad scale and most people find impossible to deal with successfully.

There are several excellent books currently on the market that confirm what we have all long suspected or known; men and women communicate differently. *Communicating with a Former Spouse* is not another look at this subject. This book serves as a tool for a specific situation, one that affects nearly half of the adult population of the United States. It is a book that reflects my personal experience and what others, who are divorced, have discovered; a number of empowering insights in the painful process of our breakups. It is my hope that sharing these insights will alleviate some of the pain that men and women experience, and bring about a better understanding of themselves and their former spouses.

After divorce, our relationship is no longer an intimate one. It is what is left of a once intimate union.

## Communicating with a Former Spouse

Communication between formerly intimate people takes a sudden twist with the finality of divorce, and people find they are unable to cope effectively because of intense personal feelings that are not resolved. We must acknowledge that we are not trying to patch up a marriage but will work to create a new relationship. Our married relationship is in the past. Some people try to reestablish the friendship that existed before the marriage, while others look at it as a business relationship for the sake of their children. Many people would be content with a civil conversation on a limited basis. In any case, improved communication with a former spouse leads to greater personal happiness.

What most former partners lack is effective communication. Supplying this simple need will diminish conflict and expand inner peace for so many of us. Generally, at present, there are a variety of common responses in relating with a former spouse. Some people impose themselves on their former spouses, while others withdraw entirely, refusing any communication. Both extremes, as well as those in the middle of the spectrum, are the best starting place for taking steps to promote a healthy new relationship, a new type of relationship . . . one that can exist between former spouses.

## "EX"

Sometimes imparting a private or negative force.

## "X"

To delete or cancel/ x out the error.

## About the Title

*Communicating with a Former Spouse* evolved from the original question, "How does one communicate with an ex-wife?" This led to, "How to Communicate with an ex-wife," and "How to Communicate with an Ex."

There are two thoughts I pondered that encouraged me to do some research. The first, is that some people, including myself, do not like to be told "how to" do anything. Second, is that "ex" has a negative connotation. "Ex" and "X" impart a negative feeling or thought to whatever we attach it to, in this case, a former spouse. It not only attaches a negative thought to our former spouse, it promotes negativity towards all family members directly connected. Why do people have to be an "ex"? Why do I have an ex-wife, ex-mother-in-law, ex-father-in-law, ex-sister-in-law, etc.? What did these people do to deserve a negative title?

Think about the definitions of EX and X on the previous page. Now think about the definition of "former": occurring earlier in time.

There are many people who speak about how important the environment is to them, the significance of whom they have as friends, and the value of positive influences in their lives. Most people know the importance of positive inner dialogue. I began to understand the importance of expanding positive inner dialogue and applying this kind of thinking to the realm of a former spouse. The interesting thing is that most people I speak to agree that the term "ex" bears negative feelings. By changing our language while communicating about our former spouse, we begin to change our perception of them and we experience a change in ourselves. A good example of this is the day I met to share this idea with my younger daughter's mother.

When I explained the importance and what I perceived as valuable in changing the term "ex" to "former" she agreed. She made it a point to phone me a few days later. She told me that since we spoke, she had started using the term "former spouse". At first we felt different, ultimately, we felt good because we were freeing ourselves from negative feelings attached to "ex". Because of the positive effect on our feelings, we chose never to use the term "ex" again.

# COMMUNICATING WITH A FORMER SPOUSE

# The Beginning

One day I dropped off my younger daughter, Shayna, to her mother. At this time in my life I had been working on specific communication skills for over a year. While there is always room for improvement, there are many successes and signs of progress when we put forth our effort for self-improvement. On this specific day, I asked her mother how she was doing and how things were going. To my surprise, her responses were cold and distant. This day I realized how our relationship could use more improvement.

I thought that our communication was on a level that was mutually satisfying and more successful than that of many other former spouses we knew, but with additional effort we could improve. With that, I mounted a personal crusade to improve my level of communication with her and with the mother of my older daughter, Hollie. My personal situation, and sharing these results with those who yearn for better communication with their former spouses for the benefit of their children, became my focus. I found that while communication improved in my former spouse relationship, so did my communication in all other relationships. Work became less stressful and life in general was much more pleasant and tranquil, thus creating a much happier life for myself, and hopefully, for my former spouses in the process.

Since then, I am able to share what I have learned, and many others have shared, of "what works and what doesn't work." By examining our experiences and applying some of our ideas, we have found this information useful in improving our communication with our former spouses.

For those of you who have lived with someone, have children, never married and separated, Communicating With A Former Spouse applies to your situation too. The same information applies because this book is for the benefit and well being of all children whose parents reside in separate households.

A classic example of this is the following story shared by a single mother who never married her daughter's father.

## Communicating with a Former Spouse

Communication is never an easy thing when emotions are involved. Accomplishing it with a former partner, married or unmarried, can be even more difficult. When my former boyfriend and I separated we fought about every little thing. He and I both deliberately did and said things to hurt each other. Our conversations always ended with nasty name-calling followed by either a phone or door slamming. We both used our daughter as a weapon after we separated. He would threaten to take her away from me and I would threaten to keep him from seeing her. It was a battle that lasted for about a year, at which point we just stopped communicating with each other.

Because of our failure to communicate after we separated, my former boyfriend and our daughter never really got to know each other. It is truly a shame that they don't have many special memories of a time when she was still a little girl. It has been eight years since our separation, and now our views are not as self-centered. Since then, we have both learned to communicate and compromise. And, we both place our daughter first.

Now we communicate and work towards a common goal. That goal is to provide our daughter with two parents who love her and will be there for her. Two parents who will come together to support her. This realization of what is truly important has made the lives *of all three of us less stressful, and provides a much safer and more loving environment for the child we both cherish.*

Communicating for the sole purpose of not wanting to feel animosity, guilt, anger, or frustration is reason enough for most people to read this book. For others, it may be that they are willing to improve their communication solely for the benefit of their children. The wonderful thing about improving communication with your former partner, for whatever reason, is that as a result, it will affect other areas of your life. If your intention is to improve communication for yourself, as you become happier and less stressed, your children will experience the change in your energy. This shift will have a direct positive impact on their lives. If your intention is to create functional communication for the sake of your children's happiness, then you will experience positive results from your efforts of improvement.

Any time communication is improved the result is better relationships, thus creating a happier life for yourself and others in your life. This does not mean there will be a lack of challenges. It simply means that as a person overcomes communication obstacles they experience greater fulfillment.

Most often, the destruction of a marriage is a long process that usually causes much turmoil. Generally speaking, the destruction of a divorce is superficial, not structural. The foundation is still intact. The foundation is made up of basic values and a capacity to love another human being.

I am fortunate because my divorce did not destroy my desire and ability to love. Nothing, I believe, can ever truly separate us from our loving essence. I am grateful because I recognize that I am the one responsible for my own happiness or unhappiness, it is and always will be my choice. Even in my darkest hours, I find that I cannot extinguish the light of unconditional love I feel for my former spouses. This light illustrates that when I decide to stop my feelings of defeat and self-pity, opportunity awaits. You and I can stop feelings of hate and failure. We can choose to pick ourselves up, dust ourselves off, and start a new life. No one is going to give our life back to us; we must reclaim it.

Whatever happened in the past, it is now over. If a process of forgiveness has not occurred yet, it can start now. We must start by forgiving ourselves for the punishment we have inflicted upon ourselves. Forgiving our former spouse comes later, and is easier for most of us than true self-forgiveness. Without forgiving ourselves, we can never forgive our former spouse. We can start by forgiving ourselves for holding on to guilt, anger, and hate. These feelings are negative influences in our daily existence and draw similar negatives into all aspects of our lives. Forgiveness is addressed in chapter two. The only way to stop the cycle is to realize that it starts with us.

Some of us may never intend to forgive our former spouse. We simply put this thought in a box on a shelf, and work on improving our communication. The first step is still the same. Once we work on forgiving ourselves, we open the door to changing how we communicate with everyone.

Changing how we communicate starts now. All that is necessary is the ability to exercise a conscious decision, and then to act upon it. I cannot tell you how many times I told myself, "things are going to be different. I am going to make a wholehearted effort to move forward. I am committed to making a difference in my life." It sounded great and felt great. I thought I made a commitment, however, I lacked action.

Our new life begins when we take that first action. We need to look at what we want to create, and break it down into steps that make it appear less overwhelming. We must set goals that are realistic and be aware that the reaction to our new approach may, at first, be negative. We need to have patience. When we are accustomed to dealing with a person who acts a certain way, change, even positive change, is sometimes threatening and difficult for someone else to accept. This behavior is partly due to our responses. Our continued action and commitment to positive change will eventually lead to improved communication.

We must start with the understanding that communicating with a former spouse is the means to creating a new relationship. This relationship is not like any other we have experienced with that person or with anyone else. We are no longer married; that relationship is over. We must create a new relationship. These simple facts are often the most difficult to grasp because of unresolved or negative emotions divorce masks from our view. Some of us may end up as wonderful friends, while others may only arrive at a state of mutual tolerance. This may be a huge breakthrough from where we are currently. Every bit of progress must be viewed from the perspective of our previous relationship.

Who determines change? We do, by our actions. It is our turn to take charge of how we communicate by being receptive to new concepts and new ways of relating to the one whom was once the most important person in our world.

# I

## Divorce:
## More Difficult Than Marriage?

If it is fair to say that marriage takes a lot of energy, it is safe to say divorce is absolutely draining. Whether or not we were the ones that initiated the divorce, it is our reality that the marriage is over. Now, we can choose how we want to communicate with our former spouse. Yes, we have a choice, and our first choice in our quest to improve communication with our former loved one should be to learn how to communicate more effectively. Effective communication means to understand what works and what does not work, and apply what we learn. The contents of this book will share with you what others and myself have discovered. When it comes to your specific situation, only you will be able to discover and create what works. In other words, there are no magic incantations that solve communication problems. If

*Vincent Gerard Molina*

Reprinted with permission of King Features Syndicate.

there were "cure-alls" or if every situation was identical, there would be a single remedy for all ailing former spouse relationships. As it is, we live in a wonderfully diverse and challenging world where everyone's situation is different, and we learn by either our own mistakes, the mistakes of others, or a combination of both.

Many divorced couples I come across express how well they thought their communication was while dating and living together, whether this was short or long term. Their communication then changed after being married and, yet again, after divorce. I discovered, in a few rare cases, communication actually improved after divorce. We also hear of many couples who lived together for several years and eventually married. Often, these couples have divorced within a few years. Why?

In all cases, communication is the barometer of how well a relationship is functioning. It is also clear that a little piece of paper called a Marriage Certificate is very powerful. For many couples, the institution of marriage appears to cause communication memory loss. This seems to influence communication efforts to repel like the two opposite fields of a magnet. The harder we try to put our limited communication skills into action, the more we struggle and get nowhere.

The real point is that our communication skills are not up to the conditions and challenges of change. We need to cease trying to force communication and turn our energy to learning new ways to express ourselves. As our situations change in life, our communication skills need to change too. Many people lack the skills or forget the basic skills needed to adjust to new circumstances. We become frustrated because what has previously worked in our lives no longer does, and we tend to blame the other person rather than looking to ourselves for new ways to communicate.

## A COMMON COMMUNICATION BLUNDER

One example of the way many individuals relentlessly pursue communication strategies that do not work is the practice of escalating questioning. In an attempt to force communication, a simple question is asked and then extended to extreme lengths, in search for a satisfactory response. This can be viewed as "bullying" or "nagging" by the one being questioned, and often provokes an undesirable response.

Example:

Q: How are you doing?

A: Okay.

Q: What's going on?

A: Nothing.

Q: Are you sure?

A: Uh-huh.

Q: You seem preoccupied or something. *Are you sure you're okay?*

A: YES! Everything is FINE!

The conversation that began innocently by a simple inquiry, progressed to a battery of questions, most likely because the questions asked were not getting the questioner's desired response. Instead of effective communication, the simple and subtle trap of escalating questioning may cause a defensive reaction by the one being probed. The person being questioned becomes irritated, switches to a defensive mode, walls go up and the chance for any productive verbal expression declines rapidly.

However, from the point of view of the questioner, the answers to questions like the ones above, given deadpan or with a hint of irritation, can be wounding or lead to anger and frustration. The person responding to the inquiries may be tired and, therefore, may not be communicating clearly. The questioner is not a mind reader, does not understand the emotional responses of the other, and eventually, this leads to a breakdown in communication. Letting go of the "need to know" at that precise moment, gives the gift of unconditional support by not having expectations regarding answers to any questions that are posed.

Of course, it takes two to play the game of escalating questioning, and both parties have the power to stop functioning on automatic pilot. Instead, they may choose to actively participate in a meaningful conversation where authentic and honest communication can occur. This might include the questioner realizing that it is perhaps not the best time to talk, or it might mean that the responder takes a moment to step back from the situation and recognize that an attempt at meaningful communication is being offered by the other person. In this case, the responder might suggest a specific time that would be better for talking, or may choose to ask the questioner if there is something more important that they want to discuss.

It is also necessary to point out that we often forget that our minds need time to process feelings into thoughts, sort through everything, and then put our feelings into understandable communication. The response to a question like the one illustrated previously may be true; everything may indeed be okay, but even if it is not, regular effective and authentic communication will build trust. Eventually, the other party will be open to communicating when the time feels right. Rather than attempting to force communication, a person with good communication skills, who senses that the other person is having difficulties relating, will find ways of showing support that will help create the right atmosphere for sharing. Effective communication is more than talking. It is listening, showing support, and offering empathy.

## TRUST

Trust is something that most individuals hold sacred in a relationship. Trust creates opportunities for experiences of real intimacy to take place that fosters feelings of a deep connection. Communication plummets once trust is broken. A trusting relationship, like an overstressed suspension bridge, can be taken to its breaking point. Broken trust can result from something like a spouse giving up on a marriage out of boredom or something as devastating as an affair.

After trust has been broken or deeply violated, it is impractical for people to expect their mates to communicate effectively throughout a divorce. When trust becomes an issue and deception is prevalent, effective communication can become non-existent. Because trust relates to basic feelings of security, experiences of broken trust may result in a variety of strong emotions. These feelings interfere with our ability to communicate; yet they can be managed, allowing effective communication to occur if emotions are permitted to surface and be expressed. Managing these emotions is a question of clarity that starts with acknowledging what these emotions are, and what events created them. Becoming clear about our emotions allows us to learn how to cope with them better. This leads to a greater capacity not only to express our feelings, but also to experience them.

Broken trust causes feelings of hurt and anger. Investigating these negative emotions, create understanding that hurt and anger are words used to describe a layered network of negative feelings. A chart of these layered feelings might look something like this:

| Hurt | Anger |
| --- | --- |
| Rejection | Blame |
| Low Self-Esteem | Rejection |
| Self-Pity | Judgment |
| Anxiety | Integrity Issues |
| Depression | Anxiety |

## Communicating with a Former Spouse

In my divorce experience, it was clear that my feelings of hurt and anger affected other areas of my life. It might be putting the case too strongly to say that these negative emotions were affecting every moment, but the negative feelings and energy between my former spouse and me definitely influenced many of my daily interactions with others. Fortunately, I finally came to realize that I always have a choice in how I react to my emotions. Emotions, when explored in their depth, actually guide us to understand ourselves better which indirectly helps us to express ourselves effectively. Choosing to actively explore and address our negative feelings is something we can do for ourselves today. We must be willing to examine our feelings honestly. We can do this individually and privately in quiet reflection.

The circumstances of a divorce play a large part in determining our communication. If both parties of a marriage agree to a divorce, then communicating can be easier because there is at least an agreement that the marital relationship is over. Neither party shares the same experiences and feelings if only one member of the couple wants a divorce. For example, from the point of view of the one who does not want a divorce, it may seem impossible to accept that the marriage has ended. Still, the other person may feel that love no longer exists in their marriage. Love is the highest form of compliment. When we have loved someone intensely and for a long time and lose him or her, our pain hurts so deeply that it feels as though it will never go away.

Emotional scars may be deep and difficult to heal. It is also difficult to accept that there may never be an answer to the question, "Why?" However, we can attempt to communicate better through our own effort or with professional counseling. There are no guarantees, just the possibility of improving communication. Not doing anything simply promotes our current experience. This can lead to bitterness and heavy emotional baggage that will be carried into all future intimate relationships. Former spouses have spent enough time together for each to pre-judge how the other is going to react to a specific situation. When we converse with our former spouse, wouldn't it be quite an accomplishment to obtain new positive levels of communication with honest listening, honest response, and no pre-judging? This kind of positive communication makes it possible to build trust in our new relationship as former marital partners.

## OVERCOMING EXPECTATIONS AND PATTERNS

*Expect nothing; live frugally on surprise.*
—Alice Walker

One definition of the word "expect" is "to think or suppose." If we have a particular expectation of an outcome such as how a person should respond or act, we are in danger of being judgmental. The word "should" is a signpost of judgement because it infers that we are holding another person to our own personal perceptions and values. This is often a not-so-subtle effort to control. It is an understandable response to a situation that feels unmanageable or overwhelming. For example, many of us think that our former spouses should act or respond a certain way. Yet, sometimes the unbelievable truth is that the choices we all make are in some way right for us at the time, or we would not make them. Learning to let go of our expectations of others is a large step towards unconditional, positive relating.

Expectations are not limited to expecting a positive response because that is want, *heaven forbid if we don't get what we want.* When a relationship has reached the point of "nothing is working," the tendency is to expect the worst. This is illustrated well by a woman who resides on the West Coast.

*Vincent Gerard Molina*

### Dave

© 1996 Tribune Media Services, Inc. All Rights Reserved. Reprint with permission.

*... In the black days that preceded the divorce, I couldn't have believed that any further communication would be of any benefit. There was nothing we agreed upon, except that we both wanted out of the relationship. In retrospect, I can see how we got to a place of expecting the worst, and the worst showed up! The main thing that was missing from my marriage was a clear idea of what commitment to communication was ...*

Improved communication with a former spouse is often hampered by the fact that individuals set themselves up, not so much by having set expectations, but by not being receptive to a response for which they are unprepared. This is important to note because each verbal exchange adds to a relationship's shape and history, and how a person reacts to a response from a former spouse will influence future communication.

In working toward more effective communication with our former spouses we are repeatedly challenged to try new approaches and confront our personal issues. Old patterns or habits are hard to break, and unless we improve on those that do not work in our lives, we will continue to get the same results over and over again. This rule applies for all aspects of life, communicating with our former spouses are no exception. The interesting thing is that when we identify what does not work, most of us never replace old habits with new, productive ones. If we find that our current communication is not working for us, then we may want to make a list of "what works and what doesn't." My guess is that most "what works" list would be shorter than the "what doesn't work" list. So, let us try a more positive approach—let us try something different! We will look at this more closely in chapter six.

Just as our habitual patterns bind our communication efforts, the preconceived notion of what divorce should be, contributes too much of the dissent in our former spouse relationships. Perhaps, because of the negative feelings that so many others have experienced in divorce, we believe that we, too, must feel anger, bitterness, resentment, or vengefulness. Another possibility is that the stereotypical "angry" roles in divorce represent the limits we place on what we believe is possible in relationships between former spouses. The typical scenario is for divorced partners to slip into a judgement mode; judgment leads to the disintegration of communication. If we are feeling betrayed or resentful, how does this benefit us? Do we communicate hate for that person for the rest of our lives? Are we going to continue to ponder the details of betrayal, or of our shattered dreams?

In terms of creating new happiness for ourselves after divorce, living life daily with hate in our hearts will only cause us to attract the same; whatever we give, we will receive. Remember that we do not have to like our former spouse's lifestyle, thought processes, or choices. We do not ever have to condone what happened during our marriage or divorce. Working toward mutual respect is the minimum requirement for being able to communicate more effectively with a former spouse. We must learn to have and show respect for each other's privacy and respect for each other's life. More importantly, if our marriage has produced new life, our focus should be on our children's future always. We must communicate on a level that will bring honor, love, and respect to our children. We must also realize that our children's mental health and spiritual growth may be jeopardized when we display selfish and stubborn behavior because we are too proud to let go of the past.

Society teaches us to live in regret. "Victim" mentalities are plentiful. Self-pity is created by rejection; this causes or contributes to low self-esteem. When self-worth has degenerated, our tendency is to blame others when in reality we need to take responsibility for our lives. The choices we made in the past makes us co-creators of our present reality. We are responsible for making our choices that determine our destination. It is normal to regret choices that have proven to be unwise or ill advised. It is also understandable that we are disappointed for choices made by others that have affected us in unpleasant ways. Blame, however, whether directed at another person or us is not the answer.

If we pay close attention to the answers we hear when we respond to the question, "What is the quality of our conversation with our former spouse?" we will notice a pattern. Responses will start with some form of blame about why communication is poor or almost nonexistent. When our current discourse is not working, there is generally a shared responsibility for the breakdown, as well as an equal opportunity for each of us to improve our situation. Even when we feel that we have tried everything, a quick inventory will usually reveal that not every avenue to improved communication has been exhausted. When we are truly committed to our mission we will find the answers.

This is demonstrated in the relationship I have with the mother of my youngest daughter, Shayna. Although we may not agree on certain things, a common ground has been established that provides a mutually satisfying environment. While it has taken a very long time for us to come to this point, it was truly worth the effort. There were, of course, many hard lessons to be learned along the way. One important lesson I learned was not to expect any acknowledgment from my former spouse because that expectation affected our communication and, usually, resulted in my feeling disappointed.

For example, for a long time, I felt great resentment for what I perceived as "cold" conversations that were taking place. I felt that I had put so much effort into being more understanding and less judgmental, yet there was no response. "Why?" I asked myself over and over, "Why couldn't she acknowledge my efforts?" In my moments of great self- pity, I wondered, "Why didn't she at least treat me like a fellow human being?" I did not understand her lack of response or ill treatment of me; after all, we were once friends, companions, and lovers. Finally, after letting go of all my expectations and allowing her to be who she is, the sky opened up, a ray of light came down, and one day out of the blue, she told me that she noticed I had changed. This valuable lesson taught me that "expectation" is another word for "judgement." I also learned that my need for her to acknowledge me kept us from relating our feelings effectively. I wanted something and when I did not get it, my disappointment affected my attitude that resulted in deficient communication with my former spouse.

Respecting ourselves enough to create harmony in our lives come from wanting a life of non-judgement and acceptance. Disharmony occurs when we fail to nurture our relationships and, consequently, we find ourselves feeling disconnected. In order to nurture our relationships, we must go through the process of coming to understand our relationships. This must start with willingness and desire to establish functional and artful communication. Notice I said, "functional" and "artful." What is my definition of functional communication? Whatever works to the benefit of both parties. Artful communication is when we are connecting to another human being in an authentic way that also creates mutually satisfying and harmonious outcomes. It nurtures the heart and expands the spirit.

A personal story comes to mind that reflects how nurturing functional and artful communication may lead to unexpected empathy and cooperation between former spouses. It was over Christmas Holiday, and my oldest daughter, Hollie and I were due to spend our first Christmas together in two years. We share a special connection during this season because our birthdays are both within a week of Christmas day. It was also during a time in Hollie's life when she began to express a strong desire to spend more time with me. She was turning eleven years old and on the verge of becoming a young lady. At her mother's request, I arranged Hollie's travel times so she could return home in time to attend her grandfather's retirement party.

Two weeks before Hollie's trip, her mother informed me that her father was taken to the hospital with chest pains. Although a heart attack had not been diagnosed, his hospitalization created an emotional disturbance for their family. I was no exception. Upon hearing this news, my inner dialogue was, "Oh no, Hollie's not coming!" My fear was balanced in a matter of seconds by my realization that Hollie needed to be with her family. I told her mother that it would probably be a good idea if Hollie stayed home. Her mother responded by saying it was not necessary because Hollie's grandfather was going to be okay. This selfless exchange was a new high point in our communication after years of having a confrontational relationship. However, that is not the end of the story.

Hollie had always flown unaccompanied when coming to visit me. I decided to surprise her this time and scheduled a business trip that would allow me to be on her flight to Hawaii. It was going to be a Christmas gift she would not forget. I even refrained from telling her mother. Two days before flying, I was unable to contact Hollie, or her family. Since I had not heard anything different, I showed up at the airport ready to spring my surprise. I found her mother; the first thing out of her mouth was that her father just had quadruple bypass surgery. Suddenly, my surprise seemed trivial. My heart sank. All that was important now was his well being and the effect it was having on everyone.

Without hesitation my former spouse said it was still okay for Hollie to travel. I was overcome with gratitude and a sense of how far our relationship as former spouses had progressed. Twice I was presented with news that seemed to jeopardize the long-awaited holiday with my daughter. Each time my former spouse had immediately reassured me that the trip was still on as planned. In many ways, these exchanges were tests of our growing new relationship and demonstrate the effort we put forth. It took commitment and continuous effort to improve our relationship. Now we are free of our former feelings of blame and resentment, and communicate in a way that is healthy and positive for everyone involved.

Opening our hearts and souls and having compassion for our former spouses is a difficult thing for us to imagine. The truth of the matter is that we have revealed the contents of our hearts many times before, in the early stages of our previous relationship with this person and throughout our marriage. What we need to remember is that, as the saying goes, "we are spiritual beings having human experiences," not the other way around. Seeing a former spouse as another spiritual being helps us to surrender our self-righteousness and allows us to become unselfish givers. This also allows us to create a way of being that attracts a higher level of spiritual relationships. The best relationships come from planting healthy seeds in fertile soil and then nurturing them to a fruitful harvest. What kinds of seeds have you been planting?

Communication is easily taken for granted in all relationships. This is largely because we often mistake communication as conversation associated with our daily living. Effective communication requires attentiveness to the importance of each exchange between partners to include: words, physical gestures, tone of voice, and mood. Marital problems develop as communication weakens between parties. Problems become compounded and may result in severe marital strain and, ultimately, divorce.

In my own case, I feel my second marriage ended because our communication was severed following a crisis point, not because of the crisis itself. This, I discovered, is common. When a crisis point is reached, even something as serious as an affair that has been exposed, there may be a complete breakdown in communication. Suddenly, there is no common language at all or, perhaps, there is only hostile language. However, more than likely, the shift in communication has not been so sudden as it appears. For example, there is regression from speaking the same language to using slightly different foreign accents and, finally, to using languages that seem to originate from different planets. We are left wondering if aliens abducted the other person!

The same applies when communicating with a former spouse. We quite often find ourselves having lost common language. Working our way back to functional and artful communication is important not only for our own personal growth and happiness, but also for the benefit of our children. It is hard to comprehend that we are struggling to coexist peacefully with a person who was once our closest confidant. Improving our communication with this person may help us to understand how things developed to where they are today. However, this is not the point. The point is that positive forms of communication will improve our lives and the lives of our children.

Once positive communication is restored it is acceptable to ask a question that may have been unthinkable in the alien language phase. Is it possible that if we had better communication skills early on, our marriage might have been saved? Although this question is probably unanswerable, it does illustrate the power and importance of possessing healthy communication skills.

For those who went to marriage counseling such a question may be less significant than it is for those who did not want to, or could not seek counseling. Unfortunately, one partner suggesting counseling for both is often met with a strong negative reaction. For many of us, counseling, or seeking any kind of help, is viewed as personal failure, or as a sign that the parties involved, and not their relationship, are broken or deficient. Counseling should be viewed and embraced as a helping tool to address issues and help put those issues into perspective. Counseling helps provide both parties with a better understanding of themselves, each other, and their relationship. Counseling also remains an option for former spouses who accept their divorce, and wish to learn how to improve their relationship with each other for the benefit of their children.

More than anything else, creating a new relationship with a former spouse teaches us that communication often requires work and learning new skills. When our emphasis is on achieving a mutually satisfying relationship, it seems even the most antagonistic relationships can be transformed into relationships with improved understanding and respect. This is a hopeful statement because it means that the life of a divorced person does not have to be weighted down by frustration and resentment.

# GOAL

*A desired result or purpose; objective;*

*The result of achievement toward which effort is directed; aim; end.*

# II

## Goals After Marriage

Did you hear the one about the spouse who left the other because of values? They valued being right more than they valued their relationship. No, this is not meant to be funny. Yet, when we pause to think about it, how often have we focused more on being right than on honestly trying to communicate in our relationship with our former spouse? A wise person once said, "I'd rather be rich than be right." These words point out that being right does not necessarily translate into success in business or love.

Being rich, whether in love, friendships, spiritually, or financially means we know how to cooperate and work together despite differences in style, perception, and understanding. The ability to allow people to have their beliefs, whether we perceive them to be right or wrong, does not have to compromise our integrity. Acknowledging a person's feelings and thoughts without judgment signifies respect for that person, not agreement with their beliefs. We need to understand that by acknowledging another person's point of view respect can be established, and a richer relationship can form. Power struggles are created when people attempt to impose their values and points of view upon each other.

Our perception of what is right is dictated by our system of established values. These include personal experiences, spiritual understandings, religious beliefs, and social norms. It is a safe assumption to say that none of us will ever hold the same values. We are all products of all these influences, and their effects on us are individually unique. This is exactly why validating our former spouse's feelings is so important. Acknowledging another person's feelings as being real and important to that person is the foundation of respect. Raising our consciousness to this level of understanding creates an opportunity for a higher level of communication with our former spouse. It also teaches us about the inherent subjectivity of our own feelings of what is right or appropriate.

Of course, it is also possible that our former spouse may not agree with our feelings. Nevertheless, another person does not have the power to make us feel that we are wrong. We may feel that blame has been placed on us. We may have been told that we were wrong. The fact remains that we are the only ones who hold the power to be wrong. We are wrong when we go against our feelings and beliefs. If another person does not validate or acknowledge our feelings it does not change the worth and reality of what we feel. When we are confronted with another person's perspective, we are given the opportunity to examine our own, and it is always possible that there is validity in that person's perspective. If we remain open to improvement and give up our "need to be right" we will improve our communication with others.

Being "right" is one way to make us feel that we are on top of things because when we are right, we feel we are in control. When we are in control of a situation we can usually predict or anticipate what to expect next. Needing to be right is a reflection of insecurity, and those who bully others in this way are really expressing neediness and emotional immaturity. The truth is that everyone's feelings are real. This means that all of us are right in some way. When the other person is a former spouse, acknowledging his or her feelings can be difficult, if not impossible, if we believe that only one person can, or should be right. The richness of our relationship with our former spouse depends upon our willingness to give up our "need to be right" and surrender our self-righteousness. When we are willing do this, we create a new way of relating that is based on moving forward and, eventually, we will let go of aspects in our relationship that do not serve us well.

There are no rules stating that we have to agree with our former spouse, their lifestyle, or opinions. No one ever said in order to communicate with our former spouse we have to like them. Effective communication is a skill that is a learned behavior over time. One primary understanding necessary for communication with a former spouse is that we must learn to set aside our need and desire for personal validation. Validation is a very basic need that we require from our parents when we are children and from our mates when we are married. Remember that we are no longer married to our former spouse. If we are still looking to them for some kind of primary validation that once existed in our marriage, we must immediately take steps to find it elsewhere. It is also important for us to remember that the best place to seek validation is in the mirror.

## SETTING GOALS AND MOVING INTO ACTION

*Thought is the blossom,
Language the bud,
Action the fruit behind it.*
—Ralph Waldo Emerson

Most of us have goals and expectations when we are first married. These goals and expectations may be to buy a house, new car, or change careers. We also have expectations like being a good spouse, who is a good listener. We may aspire to be a supportive, kind, caring, loving, romantic, patient, understanding, nurturing, forgiving, and an empathetic partner. These all require constant effort and the process of bringing them into reality is just that...a process that will always evolve.

To achieve our goals and fulfill our expectations we need three things: a clear intention of our goal, a desire to achieve our result, and action. Then, we must visualize these goals and our results. We must also increase our awareness of what it will take to achieve these goals. The same is true for goals when communicating with a former spouse. We must first set the goal of achieving functional communication, then break that goal down into the stages or smaller goals that are necessary to achieve our ultimate objective.

We all know, or can at least imagine the benefits of quality communication with others. Everyday individuals say they want better communication in their relationships, but do not set goals and work to make their wishes become reality. One simple exercise for putting goals into action is to write them down on paper. For example, what would quality communication sound like to us? What are the elements of good communication that we can name? What would be our desired result? Our exercise might look something like this:

*My goal is to respond to my former spouse in a positive, supportive manner. I will remain calm in any discussion. I will pause to hear what I am being told and reserve judgment. If I am upset, I will respond with clarity and if necessary, let it be known that I need time to think about the issue before I respond. I will love my former spouse unconditionally and see them as a spiritual being. No matter what, I choose to live a life of happiness and joy. I will respect myself enough to set boundaries that allow only positive thoughts to enter my mind. I will focus on the positive aspects of all situations. All I visualize will promote peace, harmony, and love in my life and in the lives of those around me.*

Setting and achieving personal goals is something that requires internal work. Obtaining goals takes action. Action means choosing a direct and effective way of proceeding, then doing it. Often, the simplest, most direct action is the most effective. The quickest way of obtaining what we want from someone else is to ask. One mistake I made in the past was not using the words that would generate my desired result. When I changed the words I used from, "I have a favor to ask of you" or "I need," to "I have a request; my request is...," there was an immediate positive impact on my results. This simple change in my language created a positive form of relating my desires. My old way of asking for what I wanted left me, more times, than not, still wanting. Yet, it was not just the words that made the difference, it was the spirit in which I made my request. Sincerity fuels the energy needed for artful and effective communication. I found that my more direct language enabled me to feel the sincerity of my request as I spoke the words. With an adjustment here and there, my discovery about using simple and direct language became much more than a tool to use with my former spouse, it became a universal way to communicate in all areas of my life.

## STRETCHING OUR COMFORT ZONE

There are no magical words that apply to life. Interpersonal relationships are complex, when they are not functioning positively the reasons may also be complex. All too often in the past when I had difficulty in my relationship, I would listen to other people around me and tried to decipher who had the best advice. Soon I realized that most people were telling me what to do rather than sharing examples of what they had found useful in their relationship. I also found that talking with people about my situation was difficult because some people became emotionally involved in my problems. They became judgmental or biased which I perceived as negative and controlling. Some people would urge me towards vengeance, rather than a real solution. After a while, I learned not to share my situation with those who could not support me in a positive way. Relationships may be complex, but a positive, heartfelt, and supportive attitude is quite simple.

Learning to change our language and our attitude is not easy. In my case, doing something different first proved to be uncomfortable and frustrating. I remember feeling that how I was communicating was sufficient to cause positive change. Yet, if the way I was communicating was suitable, why did my results continue to disappoint me? In the end, being open to new ideas was what saved me. I allowed a door of opportunity to open once I surrendered my need to be right. Suddenly, there was an abundance of new skills for me to learn and effectively apply in my life that I had been blind to in the past.

Opportunities for change are plentiful. I could not count the number of times someone, somewhere, whether in-person or in a book, said something that made entirely good sense to me, but I rejected putting it into action because of my pride. Change was uncomfortable and I defended my inaction by telling myself that I did not need to change. Of course, taking a few steps outside of my comfort zone is what finally worked for me to obtain new and positive results. Later, I wished I had stretched myself sooner.

## "LOVE MEANS NEVER HAVING TO . . ."

One of the most interesting words in the English language is *apology*. We often say we are sorry, and want others to apologize when we feel wronged, but a sincere apology can be rare. Perhaps, the problem is that words are easy, while feelings are not. Yet without sincerity, an apology is nothing more than a manipulative way of getting one's own way or an attempt to avoid an argument. Some people view an apology as an admission of fault, but an honest apology for something we did to offend another person is an expression of love and respect.

Apologizing can become habitual. Habitual apologizing may be a signal of possible self-esteem issues and problems with expression. In my own case, there were many, many times in my marriage that I found myself apologizing in one way or another. This was not at the beginning of the marriage, but rather towards the end, before our breakup. Looking back, I can identify this as a missed warning sign. No matter what I said or did, I ended up apologizing. I thought I was not good enough, thoughts of not being able to do anything right crept into my psyche. It was as if everything went wrong, or whatever I said was wrong. My communication began to deteriorate because I feared saying the wrong thing at the wrong time. Every moment I felt like I was walking on eggshells. I was afraid to say anything out of fear of being misinterpreted. Regardless of how humble, sincere and calm I was, it seemed what I said only made matters worse. Eventually, in my frustration, I began to feel resentment taking hold of me. My communication gradually took on an insensitive tone that my former spouse justifiably perceived as negative and responded to in kind. In turn, my perception that she did not really understand me became my truth.

One thing many people have discovered is that sometimes we can do everything in our power and it will never be good enough for someone else. One reason for this is that there are occasions when things, unbeknownst to us, are happening to someone else. These things often do not concern the one who is left in the dark. Yet, how we decide to respond to someone will have a direct impact on future communication with that person. We need to realize that whatever distress our former spouse is experiencing can only be resolved through their own efforts.

When communicating with our former spouse, like anyone else, we need to be aware that his or her abruptness with us may not necessarily be a personal attack. It may be a result of their suffering from some disappointment, or possibly, guilt. Many things in life may never be understood or resolved. Remembering our responsibility to communicate as effectively as we can does not mean we will not experience frustration and setbacks.

## CHANGING OUR COMMUNICATION DIET

*It's never too late—in fiction or in life—to revise.*

—Nancy Thayer

Just as our bodies respond to the different types of food we eat, our relationships respond to the type of communication we use. By nourishing our bodies on a regular basis, balance is maintained to ensure good health. The same is true when we are speaking of communicating with a former spouse. When feeding our relationship an unbalanced diet consisting of toxic words, unhealthy expression develops. If we do not feed it enough of the right ingredients, communication weakens and our relationship becomes susceptible to poor health.

Initially, feeding our relationship with large doses of the right communication caused an uneasy feeling for my former spouse because it sounded too good to be true. When I first implemented new and positive ways of communicating, she did not trust me. Just as we keep our bodies healthy with a balance of the right nourishment, constantly using the right language and thoughts, create a balance that fosters positive communication in our relationships.

As communication and our relationship with a former spouse improve, more energy becomes available to us for other concerns. This new energy allows us to receive more positive influences in our lives that promote growth in many areas. We are then able to express our feelings with more clarity and less emotional upset. This increased facility for emotional exchange allows our relationship to reach new levels of communication that promotes cooperation between parties. It is fascinating to see that when we demonstrate positive qualities that we have not previously displayed, a subtle shift will occur with our former spouse, one that we may not notice immediately.

Recognizing that any positive change we make in our lives is important, however our new communication may, at first, cause some frustration for our former spouse. I believe there are two primary causes for this reaction. The first is a simple non-belief in the reality and durability of the changes that we are making in our effort to improve.

The second source of frustration probably evokes feelings of, "Why has it taken so long for you to do this? Why Now? Why didn't this happen during our marriage?" Just as practicing new ways of communicating is a process for us, adapting to our changes is also a process for our former spouse. We must learn to flick off negative reactions such as, "You'll never change," or "What do you think you're going to get out of this?" We need to remember that our former spouse's perception of us is based on a period in our lives when there were more negative feelings than positive ones. The bitterness of the past may, for a time, color the perception of our present action until the sincerity of our new behavior of interacting is recognized.

## RED ANTS

The kind of internal change necessary for rescuing ourselves from the painful confusion of divorce can be frightening, especially, when we are in a state of crisis and doing all we can do just to keep ourselves together. Many of us have firsthand experience of such crisis management from our marriages. When a relationship reaches a level of crisis the confusion experienced feels overwhelming. No matter what we do the situation seems to worsen. It is as if we were stuck on a runaway train, hell-bent for destruction. We hang on, close our eyes and hope to survive an inevitable crash. Naturally, the idea is to avoid such situations, but when everything reaches full-blown disaster levels, the next best thing to do is to understand that a crisis is also an opportunity for lasting change. This means having the courage and presence of mind to step back from the situation and realize we have contributed to the creation of the mess in which we find ourselves. We also must acknowledge that we have the power to create a different and positive reality. A personal story from my childhood serves as a reminder for me, not only of what to do in a crisis, but also how to avoid one.

I was six years old, playing outside in back of my father's restaurant. There was a green grassy area with a picnic table for people to take their meals and enjoy the warmth of the Hawaiian sunshine. My sister, Lee Ann, and I were playing on the grass with our puppy, Heidi. It was a carefree afternoon of fun and laughter.

While we were playing, Lee Ann noticed a red ant on her and quickly flicked it off. These red ants were the ones that bite and produce a reaction that is irritating from one ant and painful from many. As we continued to play, more ants appeared. Before I knew what was happening, Lee Ann was screaming, yelling that my pants were covered with red ants. As I looked down at the off-white pants I was wearing, I saw what looked like fiery red polka dots all over them. Moving, fiery red, polka dots!

I jumped up screaming. My mother ran out and helped me pull my pants off. Had it been one ant, fear would not have engulfed me. Panic would not have saturated my mind, and I would have known what to do. When I heard my mother's instructions, the solution was obvious; change the situation.

It turned out that I had been lying directly on top of an anthill hidden in the grass. Had I known about the anthill, I would not have been there. If there had been just a few ants, I would have known how to handle them with a clear head. Their numbers overwhelmed me and I feared the pain of their bite. I panicked, reacted with confusion, and my anxiety level soared.

Life has many "red ants" that sneak up on us. When there is only one, usually, we just flick it off. Where there are a few, we can flick them off with little irritation. But when we are overcome by a colony of red ants, we suffer from anxiety that causes us not to think clearly and we tend to make rash decisions.

There are numerous instances of "red ants" that if put into perspective, can be flicked off without a second thought. A common "red ant" while communicating with our former spouse is a difference of opinion. If we give up the "need to be right," this "red ant" can be avoided. Learning to flick these irritating things off allows us to move forward without losing momentum.

In dealing with one of my former spouses, a common "red ant" was coordinating days and times to see my older daughter, Hollie. As a father who has one girl in one state, and one in another, my time for being with both daughters is limited to Christmas and summer vacations. This was especially challenging in December, due to limited time off from school and scheduling travel with the airlines. Sometimes it meant taking Hollie out of school for a couple of days, before her official Christmas break, and this used to create conflict between her mother and me.

The source of my irritation was that Hollie's mother rarely hesitated to take her out of school when their family went on a trip. For the first few years after our divorce, when I asked to do the same, this immediately became a volatile subject because Hollie already missed so much school during the year. This grew to be an enormous "red ant" for some time until I found that expressing my feelings sincerely, from the standpoint of fairness, while remaining calm, gave me the result I desired. Eventually, the use of effective communication shrank this huge "red ant" to its normal and manageable size and it became extremely easy to flick off.

## Communicating with a Former Spouse

"Red ants" flourish in an environment of resentment. I know from personal experience that if every little thing becomes an issue in my relationship with either one of my former spouses, this will have a direct impact on our communication. There are people who choose not to let go of their anger. I have seen people become really upset because their former spouse bought a new car or went on a trip. I have even seen one person become upset with their former spouse because the other changed jobs and made more money. And, of course, many of us become annoyed when habits and behaviors that used to bother us while we were married suddenly disappear. We sit in judgment and ask, "Why couldn't they have changed when we were married?" When there is a colony of "red ants," the longer they linger, the harder they are to exterminate. The only way is to let go of our resentment.

Let us look at all the "red ants" in our lives. Which ones just need to be flicked off? Which ones have brought their friends? Do we attract them? Is a colony of "red ants" on its way? Are we totally oblivious that we are lying on an anthill? We may want to step back and examine our situation because we may be on the verge of becoming overwhelmed by a colony of biting, fiery, "red ants."

## CRIMINALS OF MARRIAGE

When we hear that someone is getting a divorce, the first thing that comes to the minds of many people is, "Did one of them have an affair?" If we hear that one did have an affair, we immediately decide which one it was before we know the facts. Sadly, it has become an automatic response that when we hear of a divorce we assume that there is another person involved. Sometimes, this is true. Even when parting from a marriage is due to irreconcilable differences, some people still view that someone, usually one party, is to blame. Many of us picture a knockdown, drawn-out legal battle, with much guilt and blame to spread around, no matter what the situation. Individuals involved in divorce, in essence, become "criminals of marriage."

For many people, the mere act of ending a marriage falls into the category of a crime. The common logic is something like, "since nothing happens out of thin air, it had to be premeditated." Family and friends become judges and juries. One spouse, the "victim," the other, the "defendant." Someone is found guilty before we know what really happened. Never will society as a whole, much less those close to us, view us in the same way.

It does not end there. The "victim" of divorce becomes a suspect as well. Some people think there must have been some action that drove their spouse away. "What did he or she do to provoke the defendant? What *didn't* they do to make their marriage work?" Suddenly, they too, are on trial and found guilty of a lesser charge. The punishment although less severe, still has an impact on how some people in society view them.

Do we think that this has an impact on how we communicate with our former spouse? Someone is guilty for leaving; the other is an accessory. Ladies and gentlemen of the jury, although being a party to a divorce is not what most people plan on when they marry, divorce is *not* a crime. Things may have been said or not said, actions taken or not taken, but unless there was some type of abuse to warrant being labeled a criminal, a divorced person is not the same as a criminal. Divorced individuals have enough going on without having their families and friends playing Judge Ito and the LA Twelve. So many people have said that they lost other relationships because of their divorce along with friendships and broken family ties. Why? People sat in judgment, or were unwilling or unable to associate with the divorced person outside of the marriage. This happened to me, and I am sure that it *has* happened to others as well. These losses can affect communication with our former spouse. Since we cannot expect society to change its point of view regarding divorce, it is up to us who have experienced divorce first-hand to change how we feel regarding the reactions of our family, friends, and society.

Crime: An act committed or committed in violation of the law.

Criminal: One who has committed a crime.

Since being a "criminal of marriage" means that we committed an act in violation of the law, and since divorce is not a crime according to man's law, it follows that maybe we violated a higher law . . . ouch! This is tough to ponder, but it may explain why certain members of society view us as criminals or outcasts and why we may tend to be so hard on ourselves. No matter what the reality of our situation, the fact remains that those of us who suffer from this perspective must learn how to forgive ourselves and others whether the condemnation is from society or from within ourselves. There is freedom from forgiveness that allows us to move forward in our lives and how we choose to relate to our former loved one. Guilt is not a good basis for communication. Shame and blame are also counterproductive when communicating.

## FORGIVENESS

*Healing is a matter of time . . .*
— Hippocrates

Forgive:

To give up all claim to punish or exact penalty for (an offense); to give up resentment against or the desire to punish; stop being angry with; pardon.

The starting point of communicating with our former spouse can only be defined by the current situation. With this in mind, we must first identify where we both are presently, and then decide where we want to be. What has come to the surface in several discussions with former spouses is the present lack of desire to forgive, refusal to forgive, and the need to be forgiven.

This issue of forgiveness seems to be one of the best starting points for those who fall into any of these categories. Forgiveness can be the first step to moving forward in a relationship that requires some sort of clarity. The hurt experienced during the breakup of a marriage can be devastating. The role we played in our previous marriage contributes to the type and level of pain experienced.

Individuals left by their partners normally experience a pain that pierces the heart. The usual sequence of feelings is: hurt, anger, hate, and for some, a desire for revenge, not to mention an entire galaxy of feelings in between, some centering around the desire to re-establish a relationship that is over. The devastation from such an experience can leave a person feeling lost, confused, or so depressed that clinical help is necessary to get through this painful process. Those who have experienced the loss of loved ones through both death and divorce have said that the feeling is somewhat similar. There are those who believe that losing their former spouse through death would have been easier to cope with than loss through divorce. For those who divorce, there is the added burden of feeling abandoned or thrown out with yesterday's garbage. For many of us, the most difficult part of our situation is to freely forgive. How can we expect to communicate effectively if we hold negative feelings in our hearts? Although forgiveness is not required in order to communicate with our former spouse, the undeniable fact is that it allows us to be much more effective in our relationship.

The flip side of the situation is that of seeking forgiveness. It may be hard for those who were left by their spouses to believe that their former partners want to be forgiven, even though they have never asked nor shown a desire for it. So, why would someone not ask to be forgiven? How about feelings of guilt? I do not know anyone who entered his or her marriage expecting it to end. When confronted with this thought, it is a possibility, and reasonable to assume that part of what some people experience is guilt. Guilt may motivate and come to control our decisions. Guilt can fuel the decision to stay in a marriage that is destined to end. Guilt can manifest as resentment, for a lack of not knowing how to deal with the feeling of guilt! Regardless of how guilt manifests itself, and whether we are even aware of it or not, most people who feel guilty yearn to be forgiven.

I remember asking someone what they believed was the milestone in improved communication with their former spouse. They said it was when they asked their former spouse for forgiveness. They were ready to receive forgiveness, but for years previously they had never asked, nor expected, to be forgiven. This allowed both of them to move on with their lives. From that day forward, communication between these two people improved dramatically.

The difference between being told that you are forgiven and soliciting forgiveness is that a person may not be ready to receive forgiveness when the other person voluntarily offers it. Willingness to bestow forgiveness and to receive it promotes acceptance and gives people an opportunity to move forward.

Forgiveness does not necessarily start with our willingness to forgive someone else. It can also start with the willingness to forgive ourselves first. Think about it for a moment. If we are the person who left the marriage, is it possible that we are holding on to feelings that are causing us to judge, or react to our former spouse and others in a manner that is unfair to them? Are we holding on to feelings of guilt that are mandating our unwillingness to communicate in a positive manner?

We may need to forgive ourselves for playing "victim," for having an overabundance of self-pity that we use to justify not moving forward with our lives. This may be why so many people have expressed an unwillingness to consider marriage again, or why some people may justify their negative feelings for the opposite sex. Forgiving ourselves for allowing us to be controlled by negative feelings that hold us back is a good place to start on our journey to forgiveness.

Forgiving ourselves is a very powerful process. Most of us need to explore and experience self-forgiveness before we are ready to forgive others. Indeed, if we are unable to forgive ourselves, how can we forgive another person or truly receive forgiveness from anyone?

### Three Types of Forgiveness

1. Forgiving Ourselves

2. The Desire to Be Forgiven

3. Forgiving Others

*Forgiving Ourselves*

Forgiving ourselves has two elements:

A. Forgiving ourselves for having hurt another person

B. Forgiving ourselves for playing the role of "victim"

*Forgiving Ourselves For Having Hurt Another Person*

Guilt for leaving a relationship, for giving up, or for having an affair all hinder communication with a former loved one. People who feel guilty tend to avoid their former spouse. Guilt is uncomfortable and being with their former spouse may make this feeling surface. Sometimes guilt manifests itself as frustration or as anger toward a former spouse when the reality is that these feelings may be directed toward us. People feeling this way may be tormented by the thought of how much their actions were against their personal, spiritual, or religious beliefs.

Once a person realizes that they did the best they could with the tools and skills they had at the time, feelings of guilt may begin to dissipate. Forgiving ourselves is a process that begins with acknowledging why we feel guilty. The next step is to stop our emotional beatings and become gentler with *us*. We should ask ourselves two questions: "Haven't we punished ourselves enough? Isn't it about time we forgive ourselves?" If we choose to ask for forgiveness, then we must forgive and love ourselves as well.

Many people have told me that when they asked for forgiveness, they did not receive it. Most of these people came to realize that this was because they had not forgiven themselves first. They realized that the focus of their attention was backwards. They thought that if they could receive forgiveness from their former spouse then they would be able to forgive themselves. However, they found that forgiveness by their former spouse was not meaningful until they forgave themselves first. I believe that when we truly forgive ourselves, we allow ourselves to ask for genuine forgiveness from the person we have hurt or offended even though in some instances, such forgiveness may still not be forthcoming.

The next step is to take action about our guilt. Most humans, for some reason, feel guilt. When most of *us* do something that hurts another person, unless we are sociopaths, we feel guilty. Yes, it is necessary to forgive *us*; however, this alone is not enough. We must demonstrate, by our actions, that we are willing to change the behavior towards the person we hurt. Obviously, the past is the past. Past actions cannot be undone. We can, however,

*Communicating with a Former Spouse*

take responsibility for them and accept that present and future actions are within our control. Making the decision to communicate in an honest and caring way with our former spouse, and following through with action, is critical to receiving true forgiveness from *us* and from the one we hurt or offended.

It must be acknowledged here, that there are cases in which the person who is deeply wounded feels victimized, and there is simply no reaching them with a sincere apology. If we have acted toward our former spouse in a manner that has shown our desire for forgiveness, and forgiveness is *not* given, it is time to move forward. We must not allow the lack of forgiveness to control our lives. Our self-forgiveness will still allow us to communicate with loving intent. Our former spouse may or may not come to forgive us at some future time, but there will always be a need for clear and honest communication whether they forgive us or not.

*Forgiving Ourselves for Playing the Role of "Victim"*

How about forgiving ourselves for playing the role of "victim"? We may have been left, or cheated on, our kids taken away from us, lost our car, house, furniture, and family pet (pet custody is a major issue for some people) too. We may feel that "he" or "she" has ruined our ability to ever have another love relationship. Our feelings affect the way we communicate with the opposite sex in general. Our feelings may also influence how we relate to workers of the opposite sex and may impact our job performance. Maybe we are so devastated that we suffer from anxiety attacks and depression. Maybe we are in counseling and unable to work or meet our financial obligations. All of this occurs because we allow ourselves to become "victims of circumstance." Note the word *allow*. It is so much easier to blame someone else or blame an event, rather than taking responsibility for our reactions to a person or event. No one likes to be taken advantage of, to feel discarded like a candy wrapper or an old piece of gum. The challenge is to take control of our lives and rise above our experience.

Rising above the role of "victim" means working on self-esteem issues. We must take responsibility for our situation. We have the ability to change our reality. We should recognize that the person who feels guilty did what they could do with the skills and tools they had at the time. Acknowledging this does not mean that we should dwell on it. We should stop feeling inadequate for the rest of our lives. If necessary, we should seek counseling to gain the coping skills that we need to take control of our lives. Having this kind of control and taking responsibility for what happens in our lives does add to our self-esteem.

Just as with the person feeling guilty, the person who is feeling like a victim cannot forgive themselves without taking some kind of action. We cannot see a new perspective on things if we sit in the same place. Forgiving ourselves for playing the role of "victim" begins with acknowledging that we have been doing just that, and only then can we move into action toward change. To leave the role of "victim" means to step through the door of self-forgiveness and accept responsibility for our lives. We assume control over our lives and outcomes when we accept responsibility for our actions.

*The Desire to Be Forgiven*

Whether soon after divorce or years past, people come to a point of self-forgiveness in their lives. This does not necessarily mean that they are okay with what happened, but rather, that they have come to terms with the fact that they did the best they could at the time, whether or not in retrospect, they feel that they were right or wrong. The desire to be forgiven is necessary for most people to have a sense of healing and closure to that part of life that was once in upheaval.

Whether or not our desire to be forgiven is sincere, it is usually evident by the reaction of our former spouse. If they refuse to forgive us, how will we respond? Is it necessary for them to forgive ourselves for us to move on with our lives? Or, is it enough to be in a space where our sincerity is a reflection of our self-forgiveness and genuine desire to be forgiven? We may want to think about how we feel about the possibility of not being forgiven. We might remember that forgiveness begins with forgiving ourselves. Once we have truly forgiven ourselves, asking for forgiveness will give us a sense of healing and closure.

*Forgiving Others*

It is not necessary to forgive our former spouse in order to communicate with them. However, it does have a direct impact on the level of communication we have with them. For some people, forgiving means condoning what transpired. For others, it means moving forward and reclaiming their lives by expressing the true nature of their spirit. For some people, forgiving is the ability to move forward without having to forget what happened. By forgiving, individuals create better lives for themselves, learning from experience. The choice to forgive usually gives a person the ability to keep balance in their life by embracing one of humanity's most wonderful expressions; love.

Forgiveness is a process that begins by looking honestly at where we are as individuals. Taking action to allow self-forgiveness leads to the desire to be forgiven by another, or to be able to forgive another. Some of us have to go through the entire process; others need only parts of the process having already accomplished one or more steps. Just remember that forgiveness, by and from others, cannot begin until forgiving ourselves is a reality.

## Dave

# III

## You See Me But Do You Hear Me?

After ten months of being separated from Shayna's mother, I promised myself I would find a way to escape from the emotional nightmare I was experiencing. I had reached my limit of unhappiness and wanted out. At first, thoughts of complete escape came to me, that old "fight or flight" response to survive, but I wanted more than survival. I wanted a relationship with Shayna, because we are a part of each other and she deserves all that I can give to her.

I decided to fight. However, I was not going to fight blindly against an opponent I could not even name. Of course, it was tempting to blame everything on my former spouse but that did not necessarily ring true. I could not dismiss the possibility that we were not only fighting each other, but were somehow fighting ourselves at the same time. In hindsight, I believe we intuitively knew that our current communication skills and habits were largely responsible for our lack of connection. Naturally, we were dealing with other personal issues, some of them were enormous, but I understood that our communication was definitely involved in everything.

My personal crusade began with my "fight" to improve myself and increase my knowledge about relationships. One of the first things I did was read a book defining the general differences between men and women. From this book, I found out many things that previously eluded me and I became aware of some things that make men and women different. I began reading additional books on relationships and communication, one after another. As time went on, my knowledge increased and with much needed practice so did my skills. It was a whole new world for me and I was glad to be learning things I wished I had learned or known at an earlier age.

Having had a taste of new knowledge in my life after such a long period of frustration, I decided that we should try counseling. I wanted so much to understand the whole picture, and for that I would need the cooperation of my soon-to-be former partner. Unfortunately, our first counseling experience was not what I had hoped. After

## Communicating with a Former Spouse

speaking to us separately and then together, the counselor told us to forget about our marriage and move on. I was furious, and convinced that he had gotten his degree from a Sunday flea market. For a hundred and twenty dollars an hour, I did not feel that I was asking too much by wanting some insight into what had gone wrong in our marriage. I was beginning to feel that we had wandered into a scene from the movie, "The Body Snatchers;" pod people were everywhere.

Finally, we met with another counselor through our church's family services. After one-on-one sessions, we went together. He introduced us to practical communication skills including suggestions on language. My former spouse made it perfectly clear that she was not trying to repair our marriage, but just improve our communication through this counseling. I felt that we finally opened some formerly closed doors that shed some light on our current problems. We had the opportunity to discover many concealed feelings we held, and having even the narrowest lines of positive communication between us made life more manageable.

Because a relationship involves more than one person, real change can only take place with good communication. Real change also requires constant effort. Only through practice will we find our way out of the darkness of anger, resentment, and confusion. When we gradually begin to shift a mountain we once thought immovable; it will positively affect the other areas of our lives. In my story, my friends and family soon noticed that my situation was no longer getting me down. They were amazed and mystified when I was no longer upset at the mention of my former spouse's name. What I learned from their reactions was how extensive the effects of my marital troubles had been on all areas of my life. I was happy to be learning and to be successfully fighting and transforming what had almost beaten me.

Of course, my struggle had only begun and I had much more to learn. One of my initial hang-ups, a place that I consistently got stuck, was that I wanted my former spouse to take my changes seriously. Even a little bit of recognition that I was growing and changing would have been enough. Then, in one of the books I was reading, an author mentioned that you must realize that your spouse (or in my case soon-to-be former spouse) will not believe you have changed over a short period of time. It sometimes takes a couple of years for someone to believe that the changes we make are permanent. Most of us have heard the words "I'm sorry, I'll change." We also know that, more times than not, it is only a temporary change.

After reading this new information, I understood that this was another area where I would have to grow if I wanted things to be different. I could not change the fact that she was not ready to acknowledge my personal growth, all I could do was change my attitude toward receiving recognition. So rather than being discouraged and thinking, "It is going to take years to convince my spouse I have learned something through my new experiences," the only thing that became important to me was to become a better person than I already was. This was a crucial step because I was now learning and growing, and as a result, I was changing for myself and not for someone else's approval.

My perspective shifted and I applied new communication skills almost without effort. I used new skills for validation and listening, and most of all, I learned to understand that whatever she was experiencing was her reality, whether I agreed or not. This one simple understanding alone was monumental because it opened my heart to greater empathy and compassion not only for her, but also for everyone in my life. As the months went by, I noticed her reactions to our conversations gradually changed. Obviously, at times, she was still uncertain and skeptical; a feeling of "proceed with caution" came from her. Nevertheless, rather than reacting defensively to what I perceived, I continued using my new skills and knowledge. These new skills became second nature for me, an automatic way of thinking and reacting in a conversation. I was aware that, from time to time, a person could, if not careful, fall back into old habits or create new negative habits. Referring to the skills I learned helped me to avoid habits that did not serve me well.

It had been five months since I started applying new communication skills to our relationship. When Shayna's mother went to speak with her attorney, it just so happened that his office was in the building where I worked. That day, to my surprise, she came to my office after her meeting and asked if she could speak with me outside. When we stepped into the hall she asked me if I would give her a hug; something that had not occurred for more than fifteen months. We talked privately. She told me she never thought that divorce would be so difficult because she was the one who wanted out of our marriage. She proceeded to tell me how her lawyer wanted her to demand specific items and rights in our divorce. He told her that if she did not follow his advice, I would have the advantage and would possibly demand specific terms that may not be in her best interest. You can imagine how difficult it was for me to listen to her story and what I thought of her lawyer. Without visibly reacting, I continued to listen.

She explained to her lawyer that she did not wish to make any demands and told him that she did not wish to pursue certain actions because she trusted me. At this point, I asked her what it was that made her feel that way, after all, we were getting a divorce. She looked me straight in the eyes and said, "If it were not for you, Vincent, we would not have the communication we have. Not me, but you."

We all know how this marriage ended, but even so, those words greatly moved me because they were the acknowledgment and recognition I had once wanted so badly. Now, when they came without expectation and directly from her heart, this became the third of the three most important gifts she had given to me. The first was marrying me; the second was our daughter.

It took five months of perseverance, determination, and most importantly, the initial decision and commitment that I was going to work on improving myself. In some way, I had laid the foundation for better communication with all the people in my life that I loved. This was an added bonus for better communication in all aspects of my life. Our communication did fluctuate for a couple of months until our divorce was final. Without question, using all my newly acquired skills helped to make our transition emotionally manageable. After the divorce, our way of relating to each other changed again. Sadly, for many reasons we never regained the ability to have intimate in-depth conversations. We did learn, however, an important lesson; even in so-called adversarial relationships, there is room for effective communication. It takes courage, and a willingness to expose our shortcomings, but when it works, this type of relating leads to real growth and healing.

## LISTENING... A LOST ART

*When angry, count to ten before you speak; if very angry, an hundred.*
—Thomas Jefferson

I consider myself a non-traditional male because talking has always been very important to me. From the reading I have done on the differences between male and female communication patterns, I have concluded that this may have something to do with the fact that I was raised primarily by my mother and sister. For a long time I thought that if I wanted to be heard, I had to talk a lot (those who have known me for years are nodding their heads emphatically right now). In my second marriage, my former spouse seldom talked while we were married; at least that is what it felt like from my perspective. This baffled me because it seemed unnatural to me. My attitude was that if she really wanted to be heard, then why did she do so very little talking about the things that were important to her? It seemed to me that a full discussion and detailed explanation was necessary to achieve clear communication. I thought that the more said, the better.

Eventually, I realized that not only did my insistence on talking become insulting to her, it created frustration for both of us.

Talk...Talk...Talk...Talk...Talk...Talk...Talk...

This is not, I repeat, this is NOT the answer to clear communication. It seemed my former spouse and I rarely heard each other, no matter how much we talked. In fact our conversations probably sounded like:

Blah...Blah...Blah...Blah...Blah...Blah...Blah.

Oh sure, there were times when we heard each other, and it is also probably safe to say, based on our results, that over time we became increasingly lax in our listening skills. So, if this can occur in a marriage, how much do we listen to our former loved ones now? Typically, we do not even want to converse with them, and this promotes problems. Even if we really do hear what they are saying, sometimes we simply choose not to deal with what we are hearing. Yet, often there are things said by our former spouses that have more value than we can imagine. Unfortunately, because of our inability or unwillingness to hear what they are really saying, we miss the actual message. We need to keep in mind that things our former spouses tell us are often keys to a more harmonious relationship.

Of course, many messages passed back and forth in a conversation are never really stated in words. Learning to "read between the lines," for example, is a skill that some people expect others to have received genetically. In fact, "reading between the lines" is something that many of us hear about, but no one ever teaches us. There is not a course offered in school on *How to Read between the Lines*. What does "read between the lines," mean anyway? Does it mean that words spoken by someone have a different, hidden meaning behind them? Is it all about interpreting tone of voice or body language? Could it be that it requires using what we know as male "gut feeling" or female "intuition" to figure out the meaning that someone is really trying to convey? Is "reading between the lines" supposed to be a guessing game until we get it right? The real question is, "Why should anyone have to go through all of this just to understand what someone is trying to say to us?"

When we feel that we are missing an important message in a conversation, *we probably are*. We can then proceed through the mysterious process of learning to "read between the lines," or we can choose to be an active listener. I suggest that becoming an active listener is easier and far more effective. The simplest way to be an active listener is to practice listening to what is being said with an open heart, without pre-judging, and without figuring out what we are going to say next while the other person is talking. Then, once the other person has finished speaking, we repeat to him or her exactly what we heard. This demonstrates that we are listening, and that means we are progressing. I have spoken to many individuals who have used this common communication technique in their current relationship and with their former spouses; they have all reported that it has helped them to understand the other person better. In addition, these communication techniques have helped their former spouses to understand that they were not conveying what they were really trying to say. Active listening is effective. It creates an opportunity for the speaker, who may not have gotten their message across, to try again. The listener is given another chance to hear and understand the message that is meant to be heard.

Active listening is especially important when dealing with emotionally charged conversations. To exercise this skill, it is necessary that while someone else is speaking, we as the listener must focus on what is being said at that moment. Many times our energy is placed solely on our point of view and what we want to say and we miss hearing what anyone else is trying to convey to us. When asked, most divorced people I speak with tell me that when looking back on their marriages they wish that they would have listened more to their former loved ones. In regard to their current conversation with their former spouses, they recognize that listening more closely improves the quality of relating to each other while developing a more harmonious relationship.

## THERE IS MORE THAN ONE ROAD TO TRAVEL

How many ways are there to get from one point to another? Geographically speaking, air, sea, and land are ways of travel. These specific modes of transportation include: airplane, helicopter, jet, hot air balloon, sailboat, jet ski, kayak, canoe, swimming, car, truck, bicycle, moped, motorcycle, bus, taxicab, hitchhiking, walking, and in-line skating. Depending on where we are going, there are sometimes several routes to get from one point to another. The message here is that there are many ways to reach our travel destination as there are many ways for obtaining our goals for improved communication and personal growth. With allowance for personal preferences and efficiency, some established ways for reaching our goals include coaching, counseling, personal study, and honest self-reflection. These offer us ways to our chosen destinations.

Generally speaking, we are all relatively willing to accept responsibility for past mistakes and navigational errors made along our way that led us to where we are now. What is often quite difficult, however, is adjusting to, and accepting choices that others make in reaching their destinations. Whether it is how to reach an actual physical location, perform a task, or live our lives, we often have a tendency to stand in judgment over others who choose to do things differently from how we would choose to do them.

What gets in the way of accepting the paths of others? For the most part, it is the "need to be right," along with a belief system that insists on "the way things should be." In the bigger picture, for example, is it really that important that we agree on our route for getting through town during rush hour traffic? Whatever the situation, is it possible for us to take a step back and recognize that our choice is but one of many? If it is best for us does that mean that it is best for all? Learning to accept and adapt to the different choices that others make is a step in the direction of real intimacy, or even just getting along. At the very least, we need to recognize that our "need to be right" creates a burden for others in our life.

It is not especially profound to realize that our "need to be right" is in direct conflict with our willingness and ability to learn from others. In addition, our degree of willingness to learn from others, and to recognize how our actions affect those around us, allows us insight to the degree we may be willing to accept another person's differences. In my own story of self-improvement, when I finally learned to accept another person's difference in personal style, I could accept that using different means to get the same results was okay for my former spouse and me. What a relief that was because I no longer had to possess an expectation of how something was "supposed" to be done. Accepting differences is another step toward self-liberation and mutual respect.

My first lesson came while attending counseling during my separation with Shayna's mother. While investigating my need to control certain areas of our relationship, I discovered an interesting reality; there is more than one road to any destination. To many people, this may not sound like a "stop-the-presses" realization, but for me it was. Discovering that I had a need to control areas of our relationship was extremely difficult for me to face, partly because I could not accept that I was so unaware of my motivations and behavior. When the counselor brought up my controlling behavior, I got really upset and went into a state of denial. Of course, I thought, he was wrong. The thought that I was a "control freak" was unacceptable. Later I came to learn: "the bigger the alarm, the bigger the fire." What finally made it clear to me that I had control issues is an example of a very simple occurrence that was quite subtle but, nonetheless, affected our marital relationship.

Shayna's mother wanted to cook dinner one evening. She seldom cooked and wanted to show her love for me by preparing a wonderful meal. I offered to assist her in the preparation of the meal but she declined and said that it was not necessary. I insisted, and she reluctantly accepted my help.

She pulled out the pots and pans, cutting board, and utensils she was going to use. Just when she was about to start preparing the vegetables, I mentioned, that they should be washed first. At the time this seemed insignificant, but it was the second mistake that evening; the first, of course, was my insistence that I help in the kitchen. When she began to cut the vegetables, I noticed that she was having a little difficulty, so I continued to explain to her the "right" or "proper" way to cut them. She became defensive, and to justify myself, I told her that all I was doing was trying to help by showing her an easier way to do the task at hand. One thing led to another. She voiced how I was "right" all of the time and she was "wrong." She went on to say that my way was "always the best way." Naturally, I too, became defensive.

Dinner that night did not taste as good as it should have because of the bad taste left in the kitchen during its preparation. The sad thing is that this pattern had been a part of our household for some time, and even when things did not escalate, my behavior continued to add layer upon layer of resentment to her feelings toward me. My "need to be right" was not the only reason our marriage ended, however, my controlling behavior was chipping away at whatever love and intimate connection was holding our marriage together. My major lesson; there is more than one way to a destination. Giving up my "need to be right" allowed me to accept this fact.

As a "controller" in recovery, I find it interesting at times to observe the same behavior in others. I recognize that I was not always that way in our marriage. I can trace my controlling behavior back to primarily the latter half of the marriage, when a breakdown in communication generated my fear and insecurity. Of course, at that moment in my life, I thought that my way was the best way. At the time, I had no conscious awareness of what I was thinking. It started with a very simple, and for me, obvious point; "my way is better" conveyed, "your way is wrong." In hindsight, what I see as the most dangerous aspect of such an attitude and behavior is that they are largely unconscious. Controllers are the last to recognize his or her behavior because the reasons for it lie buried several layers below their consciousness. This is another reason why certain types of counseling are so effective. Counseling allows our behaviors and attitudes to be mirrored back to us so that we can see a clearer picture of ourselves, and this affords us the opportunity to move on from places where we are currently stuck.

Once we give up the need to control a situation or conversation, doors of opportunity open for us. This permits us to begin listening and accepting. Only then are we able to process the information given to us rather than remaining behind a door, deaf and with a "need to be right." The "need to be right" destroys any possibility of positive or effective communication between people.

## Communicating with a Former Spouse

### Dave

© 1996 Tribune Media Services, Inc. All Rights Reserved.
Reprint with permission.

Even if we are right, what are we willing to sacrifice to be right? I have learned that the price tag is high.

Think about the relationships we have possibly jeopardized because of our need to be right. When communication does not work with our former spouse, it will in all likelihood have a direct impact on our relationship with our children. Saying that we will never be perfect is safe, all we can do is keep learning and never stop trying. More than likely we will never be right every time. The liberation we will experience is well worth the painful recognition of our controlling behavior.

## SETTING BOUNDARIES FOR MANAGEABLE CHANGE

*Nothing endures but change.*
—Heraclitus

Committing ourselves to self-improvement and personal growth is an act of faith. As we improve, we increase our ability to cope with change and emotional distress. There is also a learning process that occurs as we begin to chart our course through the turbulent journey of our healing. We learn just how much change we can handle at a given time. Taking care of our emotional needs is an important part of our growth while we are going through so many changes. If we avoid unpleasant situations rather than address them, it is easy to become discouraged when we discover things have gotten out of hand. Using tools like writing down or saying affirmations are helpful. Relaxing or participating in one of our favorite activities is equally important.

After much thought and prayer, I found the strength to face the challenge of my own healing and growth. I decided once and for all that I refuse to be beaten by a person, place, or thing ever again. This personal affirmation gave me the strength to pick myself up and forge ahead. Although these words may sound defensive or confrontational, the attitude behind this affirmation was an appreciation of my own depth and self-worth. Negativity did not generate my motivation for change. On the contrary, I had a penetrating and positive desire to live a life free of any negative influence that I previously allowed to affect my well being. So every time a feeling of depression, anxiety, anger, self-pity, retaliation or regret would surface, I would repeat this affirmation:

*"I refuse to be beaten by a person, place, or thing."*

At first, I found myself saying this many times a day. Eventually, it diminished to a few times a week, to a few times a month, and finally, to the point where I could not tell you the last time I vocalized it. I am aware that there may be times in the future when I will use this or another affirmation in its place. I believe that anchoring the feeling of my affirmation in my daily life, helped that feeling to grow inside me until it became an unshakable part of my being. In fact, that is the value of an affirmation. If we honestly believe and feel our affirmation, our use of it will allow those feelings to grow inside us until vocalizing the affirmation is no longer necessary.

How we interpret our affirmations are, of course, essential to how they function for us. For example, the way my affirmation helps me with my former spouse is in my commitment to improving our communication. No matter how she responds to something I might say I am only beaten if I do not really listen to her. Likewise, no matter what she might say, I am only beaten when I do not examine and accept or decline any challenges for change that she might present to me. This is called taking control of our lives and not allowing others to direct our responses. Is it sometimes extremely difficult? Yes. Impossible? No.

We also need to be aware of just how much change we can handle without hurting ourselves and causing us to retreat rather than progress. In other words, each of us has to know where to draw the line. There is a balance we need to find and maintain between stepping forward in growth and being drained by excess emotional stress. Sometimes in our eagerness to please others and move forward in our self-improvement we step over this line and the result is a setback in our progress. In a way, the situations that force us to confront ourselves are tests to see just how clear this boundary is to us. When we do step over our boundary unwisely, we do not fail the test because this knowledge is useful for the next time; we learn just how far we can go and still take care of ourselves.

Shayna's mother and I managed to develop a post-divorce relationship that was civil and cordial, and were progressing to new levels of trust and acceptance. Receiving a call from her once a week was becoming more common. It felt really good to have her call me and then put our daughter on the phone to talk with me. Such progress in our relationship was showing up all over. For me, the payoff for sticking to improving our communication was like winning the lottery, or a jackpot on the dollar slots in a casino.

I felt euphoric each time I saw another sign of progress between us. It was like receiving an "A" on a report after initially receiving an "F." After re-doing the report the second time, I learned more. I began to feel confident and proud, but not overly so. After so much time and effort, I was aware that there would always be new challenges for me to work on. Communication, I had learned, is an on-going process between two growing and changing people. I now realized that change and new challenges are inevitable. The real difference, I suppose, was that I almost began to like my challenges because I felt more secure in myself and knew that, more than likely, nothing would ever change me back into the person I used to be. I had moved on and changes were welcome. I was, in other words, ready for a new test. A particular test of maintaining a sense of balance and crossing over my boundary comes immediately to mind.

One day, I received a page from Shayna's mother. When I called her back, she informed me that Shayna had been accepted to the private preschool. What great news! As she was filling me in on some of the details, she mentioned that the school was concerned about how we, Shayna's divorced parents, were communicating. Shayna's mother assured them that we related to each other well. The school's specific concern was for Shayna's well being. Since her mother had remarried after our divorce, they wanted to know of any potential problems at home that Shayna might be dealing with.

As we were talking, my former spouse mentioned that the preschool asked if all of us would be attending "Family Night," an orientation for the student's family to attend. Of course, she told them yes. So, naturally, I asked whom they had meant by all of us. Her reply was herself, her husband, and of course, me. "AKKK!" I felt as if I had a hairball stuck in my throat after running face first into a wall. My body was telling me that this was clearly threatening my sense of balance and what was good for me, my head was in complete agreement.

I proceeded to define my boundaries by calmly explaining that it was not possible for me to attend the program due to my unresolved feelings over our breakup, but maybe my feelings would change by the time "Family Night" arrived. It was not because I was angry with her or angry with her husband. It was due to the deep pain my heart still felt. I assured her that I would work toward being in the same room with him, but that did not necessarily mean I would ever come to like him. I just wanted to be able to support my daughter as much as possible and to continue communicating on a level that was mutually beneficial to all parties concerned.

Without question, I had many unresolved feelings toward my former spouse and her new husband. I needed more time to heal. The aftershock of having a vital part of my life, my marriage, involuntarily taken from me was something I was still struggling with. If I had agreed to go to "Family Night," I would have been putting myself in real emotional distress for something that was not absolutely necessary. I did not feel I had to prove my love and support for my daughter in this way. In fact, taking care of myself was also one way of supporting her. Before getting off the phone with my former spouse, I expressed a desire to improve our communication regarding Shayna. I requested that after returning from my next business trip, we meet in-person for a couple of hours to discuss our daughter. This was something we had not done for well over a year, but had done only briefly by phone. She agreed.

Drawing the line on what I was willing to do set some important boundaries for our relationship. Showing that I was willing to improve communication within those boundaries was important not only for myself, as a way of acknowledging my own comfort zone, but also for my former spouse. This conveyed that I was willing to support our daughter. Being true to ourselves in this way makes effective communication possible, it also prevents potential resentments that may build and cause a decline in communication. In the past, I might have decided to sacrifice my own feelings in order to show support for Shayna and to prove something to my former spouse. Keeping in mind my own best interests, as well as, the interests of others, is not only more effective, it is also more honest. This specific test of my personal boundaries was also about keeping everything in perspective in order for me to understand the real scope of my situation. In this regard, here are a few points to ponder:

1. Our former spouse is *a former spouse.* He or she should not be the focus of our energy or attention.

2. Our former spouse is a human being with a real heart and feelings.

3. Our former spouse is just one person. Remember that there are hundreds, if not thousands of people in our local community, millions in the closest metropolitan city, and almost six billion other people in the world we can also associate with.

4. If we can improve our communication with our former spouse it will have a direct influence in our other relationships.

5. Let go of judgments. They inhibit empathy and, therefore, communication.

6. When we learn new communication skills and apply them to our daily lives, they will eventually become learned behaviors that operate without our conscious attention.

7. Many of our current communication behaviors do not serve us well and are just getting us by. The energy we waste on ineffective communication can be better spent elsewhere.

8. How we choose to communicate results in how well our relationships work.

9. Happiness is a positive state of mind. In order to attract happiness, we must feel happy and emit happiness.

10. With people, like attracts like. In order to attract non-judgmental people into our lives, we have to become non-judgmental. This means loving and taking care of ourselves.

Point number seven needs further emphasis. So much of our valuable energy is wasted on ineffective communication. Effective communication is largely about getting it right the first time so that we are free of hidden agendas, resentments, or misunderstandings. This also applies to how we communicate with ourselves. An example from my experience illustrates this quite well.

Although my former spouse remarried, I kept writing our daughter's child support checks payable to her mother in my last name. Since I convinced myself that I was not 100% sure what name my former spouse was using, I chose to keep writing the checks to her in the way I always had. Of course, I always wondered what name she was using, but the whole issue became something of a game that I played with myself. I directly deposited the check into our daughter's bank account and not once had any of the bank tellers commented about to whom the check was made payable.

The game I was playing with myself was semiconscious. I realized that on some level I was resisting change. I had difficulty accepting the way things were and, indeed, this name game I created illustrated this fact. Eventually, either the bank or my former spouse would correct me. Nevertheless, until that happened, I chose to dance around with the whole thing. It was funny that after making such progress at letting go, I was still trying to hold on to something that I had absolutely no control over. Still, I was not able to see that not letting go was another form of controlling, so this game continued. Every month, when I walked into the bank the same two thoughts entered my mind: "Is the teller going to ask me about this? Should I ask the teller?" I felt very stupid, and yet I could not find the emotional strength to move forward by asking my former spouse what name she had chosen to use.

One day, I received a call from my former spouse telling me that there was a photo advertisement in one of our community newspapers of her, her mother, sister, and our daughter for a local woman's clothing store. You can imagine, as a proud dad, I wanted to see my daughter's picture in the newspaper. I picked up a copy of the paper later that day and could hardly wait to open it up to the page where this monumental picture of Shayna was located. With excitement, I turned the pages quickly and actually went right by it. Finally, I went back, turning the pages slowly until I saw my daughter. Then my eyes dropped to where they printed the names of everyone shown in the ad. Yes, here was my former spouse using her new married name. Initially, my heart sank, then to my surprise the heaviness I had long held in my heart was gone. All that stuff I was carrying was for no reason at all. All that energy I wasted. For me, this just reinforced how powerful our minds really are, and how holding on to such things only diverts and misuses our energy.

## UNEXPECTED CHALLENGES AND PAYOFFS

While in the midst of living new lives separate from our former spouse; little crises can emerge from what appears to be out of nowhere. These crises always seem to take us by surprise. Sometimes it can even feel like a truck blind-sided us. Not just any old truck, but maybe an eighteen-wheeler. By the time we recognize what is happening, our stress button has already been pushed. Our anxiety meter is in the yellow zone, and might be climbing to the red. It is easy in such situations to be at a loss for words while trying to figure out what is going on. We might ask ourselves in the heat of confrontation, "Why is this happening?" or "Who declared war?" and "Where in the heck is my shield?"

Here are two examples of an unexpected conflict with a former spouse: What is being discussed is a new issue, or it is an old one that has, for some reason, resurfaced. If it is a new issue, remember that we are at a disadvantage if it is something that is brought up to us for the first time. He or she has had time to think it over before talking about it, but we are hearing it cold. If we are having trouble getting a handle on what is being said, that is understandable. We may inform our former spouse that we have not had a chance to think about the issue, and may want to ask for more time to consider all the sides of it. If we feel pressured we should try to get as much information as we can, hold off making a decision, and schedule a time for discussing things further. Sometimes only five minutes of time alone to think will be all we will need. In the face of continuous pressure, we may choose to inform our former spouse that because this is such an important issue, we need to be certain of our best response to prevent future problems and possible misunderstandings.

If the unexpected confrontation concerns an old issue, maybe we have come to either an "unspoken arrangement" or an actual arrangement. Naturally, "unspoken arrangements" can lead to problems. If so, we could schedule a time for an in-depth discussion and take time to be as completely prepared as possible so that when the appointment time arrives, we will hopefully, end up with an arrangement that works for everyone. If this is not possible, we could schedule mediation.

If the confrontation concerns an old issue for which we already have an actual arrangement, we should not panic and think or expect the worse. What we need to do is realize that this conflict may not be about us. We could gently remind our former spouse about our previous agreement. Still, our former spouse may feel the need to re-negotiate.

Before agreeing to any meetings regarding re-negotiation of previously set arrangements, we should closely examine any concerns or objections from our former spouse. Is this flare-up truly about the issue of our agreement? If not, what is it really about? Why are we the targets? How can we resolve the issue to satisfy both parties? Reality dictates that all things have an end. Reality also dictates it will last as long as it takes to work through the real issue at hand for our former spouses and us. Depending on the kind of relationship we have with each other, we can assist in changing the shape and scope of the confrontation by applying active listening skills. We may want to mirror back what we hear and then ask simple questions like: "Is there anything else? Could there be another reason that you are upset with me? Can I share my perspective on this issue with you?" Once our former spouse understands that we are actively listening, and not just reacting, there will be a shift in our confrontation. If not, we could choose to let it go. Perhaps later we can talk when the emotional charge has lessened.

Like every other skill, learning to handle emotionally charged confrontations takes much practice for most people. Sometimes trying to keep from becoming defensive until we can think clearly is like expecting world peace. The good news is that with practice we can learn to lessen our defensiveness and reactions. The most effective way to do this is very simple: We should not take anything that our former spouse says too personally. This is much different, of course, than not taking *seriously* what your former spouse has to say. Taking things personally means that we allow what someone else says to affect our sense of self-worth. Taking others seriously means that we recognize that whatever they are feeling and experiencing is quite real.

Actually, the very good news is that our commitment to self-improvement and personal growth has payoffs. Payoffs sometimes come in the most miraculous and unpredictable ways in all of our relationships. The greatest payoff is in how we feel about ourselves every day and our ability to have healthier relationships with people we care about. In my case, one big payoff was that after three years of skills training in communication, I could tell Shayna's mother that I no longer carried any anger toward her or her new husband. More than anything, I was simply glad that she was happy. I also expressed my appreciation for our current communication and looked forward to our continued improvement. She knew that I sincerely felt what I said, and her acknowledgment of this was very important.

When I made my commitment to change and self-improve, if someone had told me that I would one day look back on that day as a high point in my life, I would not have understood them. Yet, it is the truth. Finding the inner-strength and willingness to change is a real lesson in how we are so much more than we generally allow ourselves to become. In fact, such commitment to personal change and growth is only one small fraction of all we have to offer others and ourselves.

# IV

## Support: Emotional, Physical, Financial, & Spiritual

Everyone has a right to an opinion. We may feel differently than our former spouse about a specific issue. Issues such as child support, bedtimes, friends, activities, and a multitude of subjects relating to our children have to be addressed. Unfortunately, many of us may fall into the habit of avoiding these very important issues.

Throughout the procedure of a divorce, many of us do not really understand the legal language used and how it actually affects our rights as a parent. Some of us just want to get through this chapter of our lives as quickly as possible. Some of us want to dominate the process by making sure we have control of property, money, and most importantly, our children. How did a relationship that started with two people loving each other end up in fighting over who receives how much, or control over how much a parent is allowed to see their own children? Call me an idealist, but both parents should have equal rights when it comes to their children, barring such obvious extremes as emotional, sexual, substance, or physical abuse. The whole concept of one parent receiving full custody baffles me. I am not referring to a primary living place, I am referring to the right to see a child and be a part of the decision process when it comes to major areas of their life. As Solomon pointed out thousands of years ago, it is not physically possible to cut a child in half; with each parent taking one half home to raise. The reality is that, most of the time, one parent receives primary physical custody. My hat is off to those parents who have found a way to share in their child's life without creating a knockdown drag-out, ugly environment.

Supporting each other in discovering the best way to raise our children is not always easy, because whether married or divorced, the fact remains that each parent has a preconceived notion on how they want their children raised. This may stem from how parents themselves were raised, personal value systems, and how society has and is changing. The process of expressing our opinions in this area is like everything else. We can choose to verbally slap our former spouse across the face, or express ourselves in an artful manner. This does not mean that what we say will be received with open arms. It does not mean that our wishes will be granted. However, our gentle and artful approach tremendously increases our chances of being heard. Again, our focus should be placed on the issue at hand, not the issue of how we feel about our former spouse. We need to keep our personal feelings at a healthy distance.

Support is different based on a given situation. As individuals, some of us know what our former spouse needs in order for them to feel good during a conversation. Others have yet to discover this because they have never known these needs. Some of us may refuse to listen to what is being said, or ask what the other needs. When we know what others need, we can then find a way to provide it in a way that feels good for everyone. Feeling good about supporting our former spouse may not be a constant; it does not have to be. Remember, support is different based on each situation. No one is asking us to give until it hurts. Giving should feel good. We need to look at why and how we are giving. If we think that what we give now is not appreciated or reciprocated, we may ask ourselves these questions: "Why do we keep giving? Are we giving for the purpose of receiving? Are we giving to be acknowledged? Are we working towards giving unconditionally?"

If our support is conditional, no one wins. Conditional support should be avoided. Learning to give support for the sole purpose of wanting to give alleviates adverse feelings towards our former spouse. As in many other situations, we need to set boundaries to ensure that we are giving out of our willingness to give support, rather than giving out of guilt, or a desire to get something in return, or, some other less than positive motivation on our agenda.

While training and consulting in the area of customer service, it dawned on me one day that there is a parallel relationship to that with a former spouse. If it is a basic tenet that customers are asked what they need, then we may want to ask our former spouse what it is that they need. A simple question like, "What will it take for us to relate on a level that is mutually beneficial?" This could be the start of a fulfilling relationship.

Remember: We do not have to agree with or like our former spouse's lifestyle or decisions in order to communicate with them.

The next step is to educate our former spouse as to what we need in order to keep our communication lines open and healthy. Our need could be as simple as giving us time to speak rather than cutting us off in the middle of a sentence. It is very difficult to communicate effectively when we are not given the time to ask supporting questions and express what we may need. Meeting in-person with our former spouse can benefit both parties as our newly formed relationship progresses. Meetings do not have to be long. Maybe we could get together for a cup of coffee or our favorite beverage in a mutually selected public place: a coffee shop, cafe or informal family restaurant.

In most cases, children are involved and are the lead topic, so we might discuss them first. Our goal should be to clear up questions on how to raise them in different homes without contradicting each other. The means to achieve this goal is usually the cause of disagreement. A good beginning is the recognition that both of us love our children and want what is best for them. Approached tactfully, many of our wants or goals in this area become reality because of our desire to have them fulfilled. Desire drives our inner power, and this allows us to create anything we want. These desires materialize from having a thought, putting the desire behind it, and taking action.

If we really want a better relationship with our former spouse, most of us need to change our approach because what we are currently doing, obviously, is not working. To find that new approach, we simply need to ask our former spouse questions, listen to their answers, and take action.

How our former spouse perceives us and what they feel is real for them. We should not be afraid to ask how they rate our current relationship on a scale of one to ten. It is probably not what we want to hear, however, they may surprise us. Once our question is answered, we should explore what it would take to better our current situation. This relationship is not the same one we had when we were married; our goal is not to obtain that sort of relationship, although anything is possible. Our immediate goal is to improve our communication so that our current relationship improves. If our goal is to express ourselves without yelling, swearing, demeaning each other, or to simply gain more support in a certain area, we should set one goal at a time, and take responsibility for our own actions. Our goal may be a simple one, like the ability to discuss our children's well being, education, or visitation. Anything that is a step forward is a *win* for all parties.

Striving for the best relationship possible means making concessions. It also means we must understand that our former spouse may never change and accept this fact. The important thing is that we have the desire to become a better person and do the best we can. We should seek the good qualities in our former spouse and nurture those qualities. We should focus on supporting and respecting their desires and feelings because they are real for them. When we judge them to be wrong for what they believe or feel, any wall between us becomes taller and thicker. With every negative word uttered and action taken, the wall becomes so enormous that any of our previous work must be re-done to re-establish trust and communication. If we extend kindness and understanding, we help to remove the bricks and, eventually, the wall may come down. This may take weeks, months, or even years. Once we know what type of support our former spouse needs, we can begin to take a step towards better communication and a healthier relationship.

Areas of support that repeatedly show to be of value for individuals are emotional, physical, financial, and spiritual. The following sections glance at what others have experienced. These areas may appear differently for some individuals, but for others they may be the same. We can use this information to form a comparison to what is currently happening in our lives. From this, we can draw our own conclusions about our weaknesses and strengths, and then focus on where we need to apply our energy.

## EMOTIONAL SUPPORT

Each person has what can be termed an emotional bank. This bank holds all the emotions we are capable of feeling, positive or negative. We are in charge of what is deposited or what is withdrawn. Our choice to act or react dictates how high a price we pay in expending our emotions. For example, the action of avoiding an issue or having to walk on eggshells to avoid confrontation in our relationships depletes our account. Our cost: fear, resentment, and unhappiness. Those are just the "up front" costs. If we look at the back end, we will see that emotional exhaustion affects our current relationships.

There must be more positive emotional deposits than negative for human beings to be happy. There also must be withdrawals that express a negative so that these emotions may be released. But, if we do not make positive emotional deposits, eventually, we will have depletion. Consider the consequences of a no yield and no bonus emotional account that dwindles fast. The penalty for a low balance in an emotional bank could be the absence of much needed "interest" called peace of mind.

To re-establish a healthy account, we need to make ourselves the most important person. This means being okay with who we are. Second, we need to see everyone around us as spiritual beings. This takes practice. When we work at not judging others there is an absence of negative energy that allows positive deposits to enter our emotional account.

Shifts continuously take place during all relationships, including the one with our former spouse. When we think all is well, some unexpected event may occur, throwing a new dimension into focus. Accepting the fact that change is constant helps us weather the unexpected events we come across.

If there is constant change in our relationships, then no matter how much we may try to keep things the way they are, outside influences will dictate that change occurs. How we prepare ourselves to adapt to this change is what can make the difference. Taking responsibility for what we do draws us away from blaming others for what they lack and for what they are, or are not, doing.

There were a number of times that I asked Shayna's mother to call and let me know what the doctor had to say about Shayna's health. Shayna suffered from respiratory problems and ear infections at a young age. Her condition took her to the hospital on several occasions. Shayna even had her own breathing equipment at home for when she experienced any difficulty in breathing. It became customary for me *not* to receive a call the day she went to the doctor. I experienced hurt and resentment hearing about Shayna's doctor visits after the fact. My frustration rapidly set in, and before long, I placed more emphasis on the fact that my former spouse did not call me, instead of placing emphasis on my daughter's health.

I was angry with my former spouse and used our daughter's health as the reason to justify my anger. I masked my negative feelings towards my former spouse and hid behind our daughter. I explained to my former spouse that it was important for me to receive a phone call regarding our daughter's health, however, she reacted defensively. Her response is a typical one among other people in similar situations based on their current level of communication. Once we established a more artful way of communicating we were able to contribute to each of our emotional banks in a positive and nurturing way.

There are times when Hollie's mother has many a dilemma with Hollie. From not listening to instructions to poor grades, our daughter has typical moments like most children. Her mother has borrowed my ear on more than one occasion. It has been both challenging and frustrating for me. At the same time, I know that each time I actively listen to her, I give her the emotional support she needs. Since Hollie's well being is first and foremost, my feelings about her mother must not interfere with our daughter's well being.

Many men and women allow their personal feelings towards their former spouse to get in the way of how they deal with their children. It may not be conscious, but it is common.

Currently Hollie's mother feels comfortable sharing with me personal frustrations about life, work, and family. I cannot help but be amazed at how our communication has evolved over the years. I may not always want to listen, I may not agree with, or like what she says, but the fact remains that she has feelings that are real, no matter whether I feel they are right or wrong, or, if anyone else agrees with her or not. When I realized this fact, life became a lot easier and my listening skills improved immensely. Emotional support is just one of communication's necessary nutrients that allows any relationship to flourish.

## PHYSICAL SUPPORT

*Know the right moment.*
—Diogenes Laertius

The physical aspect of a relationship with a former loved one is the hardest and, at times, the most rewarding facet of having a former spouse. You may ask, "What in the hell is he talking about?" Or better yet, you might be thinking that I am referring to sex. Not even close. I am referring to another powerful and physical three-letter word ... HUG. Some of us cannot imagine being in the same room with our former spouse, let alone touching them. The fact remains that a hug can be more powerful than words.

Hollie's mother and I were divorced for about two years when by a small miracle, I was able to put what had happened in the past, in the past. The miracle was taking back control of my life by forgiving myself for being a victim and feeling like a failure. I swore that when Hollie's mother and I married I would be married only once. I felt the need to make myself this promise because my parents were each previously divorced, my sister was divorced, and so was my brother. I discovered three things:

1) I was not supposed to have married this person in the first place.

2) I did not fail. Instead, I lacked knowledge. I simply did not know any better at the time.

3) I discovered how harshly I had judged my parents and siblings.

A divorced person is not like something broken that has to be fixed. A divorced person is not a discarded piece of trash. A divorced person has a lot to offer

## Communicating with a Former Spouse

someone else in a new love relationship. Divorced persons are worthy of another love relationship. I discovered that I loved myself and was worthy of having another love relationship. As I learned these very important lessons they became a part of my life.

I remember phoning Hollie's mother and explaining that my life was better now and looked forward to seeing her and her husband, formerly my best friend, in a month. She asked me, "Are you on drugs, or drunk?" I laughed, which did not immediately reassure her. At the same time, I understood where she was coming from because of my previous attitude and angry persona. Assuring her that I was not on any mind-altering drug, I said I would explain everything during our visit. I can only imagine what she may have thought for those next 30 days.

The moment of truth arrived on Father's Day as I drove up to their house. When I got out of my car, Hollie ran up to me and jumped into my arms. I walked up to her mother, put my arms around her, and gave her the hug that I once thought would never be possible after we divorced. Next, I hugged her husband, his eyes almost popped out of their sockets from shock. Understand two things: we were once best friends for three years, who hugged as some friends or brothers do, and, he and she ended up together while we were still married, which was the cause for him and I to cease communicating for several years.

As I am sure anyone can imagine, they had many questions for me. Hollie and I spent part of the day together. The latter part of the day we all spent together. I said to Hollie's stepfather, "I bet you are wondering what has changed for me, and why I am so willing to re-establish some form of a positive relationship with you." He admitted he did not understand because I displayed so much anger and resentment towards him and my former spouse up until this point. I did not blame him for being skeptical. It took a lot of explaining, and a lot of time passed before they understood that my words and actions were genuine. My underlying motivation to change the way I felt about them was the love I have for my daughter, Hollie. One thing is for sure, that first hug communicated trust, love, and forgiveness like no words could have ever expressed.

I do not suggest that everyone run out and hug their former spouse or their new mate, even after emotionally ready to do so. I only share this story for the fact that just like Shayna's mother asked me to hold her after she saw her attorney, there are times when physical contact is appropriate, if both parties are emotionally prepared for an intimate exchange of energy.

## FINANCIAL SUPPORT

How many of us like to financially support our former spouse and our children? How many of us actually meet our financial obligations? How many of us who receive financial support feel it is not enough money? How many of us feel it is a right, not a privilege, to be receiving money? It is simply amazing how people meet, get married, have children, get divorced, and one does not want to support their children, and the other one feels they have a right to a check. When it comes to children and financial support, some people discover that the focus shifts from a child's financial well being to their own need of financial support.

A person may not want to provide child support because of resentment, anger, and other feelings toward their former spouse. The other one may feel they cannot support their child or children without monetary assistance. On the other hand, one may feel that the money for child support may be misused and the other may feel they deserve that check.

Whether we like it or not, when these children were conceived, we took on a lifetime of responsibility and commitment. And, although these other thoughts and feelings may be valid, the fact remains that both parents share a financial responsibility to their children.

## Vincent Gerard Molina

People complain constantly about money. From the perspective of some non-custodial parents, if a former spouse is unable to take care of a child without the support of the other parent, maybe custody went to the wrong person. They may feel that the money sent should be over and above basic necessities, like icing on the cake. Some parents would be more than willing to take over full care of their child from the other parent and not ask for a dime. And yet, there are cases where some parents are unable to make it financially, due to circumstances beyond their control. Just to be clear, it is understood that people sometimes find themselves in a situation where they are unable to financially take care of their child on their own due to a divorce that seems to come out of nowhere. These people were not afforded the time they needed to prepare themselves adequately for their future, and the future of their children.

Many people were robbed the option of making their marriage work and would have done so, no matter what, because of their willingness to do what is necessary for the well being of their children. It is a scary thought that if something was to happen to the parent paying child support, that their children might suffer. If the custodial parent feels the need for financial support and is unable to raise the children without it, what would they do if the other parent were to die tomorrow? Are they prepared to financially support their children alone? What would they do? Not a pleasant thought, but a reality. These are questions for all of us to ponder.

Money is such a sensitive topic for couples. Money can be an addiction and as destructive to a relationship as drugs or alcohol. Most of us view money as a way to measure success. Money is simply a means to accomplish certain goals and to acquire material things. Many of us feel money makes us happy. Money can do a lot for us, but money does not make us happy and although this is a cliché, it is true, *happiness comes from within.*

When money becomes the focus of our communication with our former spouse, spirituality dimmers, and our focus on money can drive a wedge into our relationship. Financial commitment to our children must be an emotionally voluntary decision. Once we accept and are willing to support our children, our energy can be redirected to other areas of communicating, and to other areas of our lives. Years ago, discovering this fact allowed me to provide child support unconditionally to my daughters. Defining child support as an opportunity to provide for a child in a manner that allows a non-custodial parent to participate in their life, while not being able to participate physically, on a day-to-day basis, helps to relieve stress associated with the financial obligation. Approaching child support from this perspective generates a feeling of unconditional commitment from parent to child. What makes it difficult to hold on to this feeling, at times, is the value our former spouse may place on money. Asked about this matter, thinking it to be a settled issue, can push a former spouse away, create defensiveness, and cause barriers and thick walls to re-appear.

Some people will feel and declare that the other "can't live without my financial support," or "they count on my money to make ends meet." Most likely, these thoughts come from the energy a former spouse puts behind their words. If we experience this, we may express that if the roles were reversed, we would not count on financial support to make ends meet. Although this may or may not be true for everyone, it is "food for thought."

Understand that we are obligated to provide for our children, and more important, we should want to provide for them. We are obligated out of responsibility, and motivated by our love for our children, and should not be made to feel obligated out of guilt. Like most other things in life, when we feel forced into something that we may truly want to do, we may feel resentment and resistant. The value of providing financial support can be created if only it is communicated differently. What may create value for spouses to furnish financial support are the specific needs of their children like clothing, education, medical and dental coverage, etc.... Communicating the importance of the needs that have a direct impact on our children's current and future well being, is the most effective way to receive a desired result.

## SPIRITUAL SUPPORT

*Since we cannot change reality,
let us change the eyes which see reality.*
—Nikos Kazantzakis

Let us take a deep breath, let it out, relax, and imagine for a moment what it would be like to be living a life that is free of communication anxiety with our former spouse. Each time we need to call our former spouse we experience calmness. We are relaxed and feel peaceful. Each time we check our messages at home or work, and there is one from our former spouse, we are at ease. We can express honesty and sincerity to our former spouse that he or she deserves to be happy. Thinking of them, we no longer focus on what happened or why it happened, and instead choose to remember the wonderful things about our time together. When our former spouse's name is brought up in a conversation with our new partner, neither of us feels uncomfortable.

For some of us, this exercise may seem realistic, but for others, impossible. If we fall into the latter category, we should not despair. It can be done, and we can achieve artful communication with our former loved one, and, it will take time; we should not spend valuable time blaming ourselves or our former spouse if this does not materialize right away. Since we do not live in a perfect world of communication we need to consider being gentle with ourselves while developing new communication skills. By taking one step at a time, we can continue to make progress.

As with many other things in life, how we choose to play, whether we choose to show up consciously, will have a direct effect on our level of expression. If we sit on the sidelines and the game continues in our absence nothing changes for us. We need to get in there and play with our hearts because there is an opportunity for us all to make a difference in this world.

We should want to be the example for all parties to win. Just our participation with an open heart will have a profound effect on those around us. If we give the gift of unconditional love by recognizing we are spiritual beings, and see others as spiritual beings, we can make a difference. Making this one change has a profound effect on our communication; not only with a former spouse, but also with every other person we encounter as we journey through life.

As said before, our willingness and desire to improve this area of our lives will affect every other relationship we have. All we have to do is give in the true spirit of unconditional giving, and by doing so, we will receive those same things in return. Tenfold, it's the law!

Imagine our former spouse as nothing more than a beacon of light, no physical body, face, or name. There are not any memories to which feelings can attach themselves, and no verbal sounds that require our attention. There is only light and a feeling of positive energy running through their being.

Now, imagine having to communicate with this light and energy. How would we do it, what would we say if anything at all? Would we express ourselves through our life force, the core of our soul? Could this be the spirit we hear about? Would our words be effective, or would just a feeling, or thought convey our message?

Imagine never associating a past experience, whether verbal or physical, with our former spouse, but rather just see them as a beacon of light, a spiritual being in the present moment. No judgment, no prejudice, just a life force here on the earth. Do we think our communication can be more effective given the new way we choose to see our former spouse?

We only have to see one another for what we truly are; a life force. There has never been a child born that was seen by those around them as a bad spouse, or former spouse. We see children at birth as a blessing upon the earth and in our lives. That child of light is still there within each of us . . . within our former spouse. Even within us.

# PERSONAL:

*Of or relating to a particular person: private.*

# V

## Your Personal Life, My Personal Life: What Is Off Limits?

The road signs read: CAUTION! DO NOT ENTER! OFF LIMITS! HAZARDOUS ROAD AHEAD! Did we pay attention to these messages? Nooooooooooooo. Can we imagine how it feels to have someone who has chosen not to be in our life, or whom we have decided we do not want in our life, continuously ask us personal questions? How about sharing with us their personal life when we do not want to hear it? Well, this does happen, too often. Many of us know what I am talking about. Constant questions demonstrating a need to know about a former spouse's personal life can be viewed as nosy, or perhaps, a need to control. On the reverse side, voluntarily sharing what a wonderful life we have, and all the details, could be viewed as gloating or vindictive.

It may not necessarily be the intention of our former spouse to make us feel miserable, although there will be those instances. This may derive from a burning desire to control situations, of which they have no control in their lives. This kind of control may give them a false sense of feeling good about themselves. Remember the saying that we hear in some movies, "I'm going to make your life miserable." This line is meant to dramatize the narrative we view on screen, but in reality, this is pathetic when we hear this directed at us. Unfortunately, there are people who do not have a grip on their own life and feel the need to act out in a melodramatic way. Perhaps they are co-dependent and suffer from low self-worth. These people may count on others for their happiness. This may be illustrated by a need to know personal details about our life, or because they want us to feel as badly as they do; "misery loves company." A former spouse may feel lost without their mate. When Shayna's mother told me that there was another man in her life, my world crumbled. Later, I realized that I depended on her presence in my life; she *was* my life. I had not developed my own life and sense of self-worth beyond her, and literally depended on her for my happiness.

A developed personal life gives us a sense of independence, freedom, individuality, accomplishment, and strength. We need to set boundaries in order to prevent others from intruding in our personal lives. Former spouse relationships should honor and respect boundaries set regarding things of a personal nature. This can work if we are sincere in our endeavor to create a more harmonious environment for our children and ourselves.

I remember Hollie's mother liked to tell me everything that she, her husband, and our daughter would do, *in detail*. Every vacation, every weekend, and every function. I would hear about all the fun they had and these updates went on for a long time. I also remember the resentment I felt. How dare she share her new life with me after leaving me for my best friend? Every time I listened to these stories, I felt as though she was rubbing my face in a big pile of dog excrement. It felt like cruel and unusual punishment. I told her a number of times that I did not want to hear about her new life and she would comply, but her compliance only lasted a short time, and the cycle began again. To top it off, she would ask me questions about my personal life like, "Are you seeing someone?" She also felt a need to give me unsolicited comments like, "You will find someone," and "You need to get out there and start dating again." I wondered, *is she nuts?* I felt that she was shoving her life in my face, asking me questions about my personal life, and telling me what to do. Hello?

After months of listening to her updates, questions, and unsolicited advice, I told her again, and in no uncertain terms, that I did not want to hear the details of her life, and to please stay out of my personal life. Was I calm, cool, and collected? Not at first, in fact I remember feeling emotionally heated, but eventually, I calmly expressed how hurt I felt when she communicated these very personal things to me. Ultimately, she understood my feelings.

Sometimes, I felt that she shared her personal life as if to mock our marriage. Other times, I felt that she needed my acknowledgment that she had found the happiness that lacked in our marriage. From my point of view, what was missing was her lack of respect for my feelings and the relationship we once shared. It was as if the corpse (me) was not cold yet, and she showed up to the funeral, married. It felt like someone was squeezing lemon juice into my open wound. This is how volunteered information and unsolicited comments from our former spouse can make us feel. When former spouses share this kind of information, and delve into our personal lives, after being asked to refrain from such conversation, the more hurt and angry we may feel.

Understanding that personal lives are off limits is not limited to intrusive questions. We should realize that we must also refrain from sharing our personal life with our former spouse. Given the above example, sharing our personal life may be hurtful. Our lack of awareness and sensitivity can be perceived as if we are intentionally trying to hurt the other person. A former spouse may experience negative feelings if they have unresolved feelings of their own. This, most often, applies to a former spouse who did not want the divorce, or who suffers from guilt.

Personal lives *are* personal. Although our marriage was dissolved by a court action, feelings do not cease as easily. Sometimes things are shared for the sake of sharing. Some of us do this based on the friendship we once shared with the other person not realizing how hurtful this may be to the other. Others may ask questions to show an interest in the other person as a way to build a new relationship. However, this may feel like an invasion of privacy and may create negative results.

Our experience is based on our current relationship with our former spouse to include unresolved feelings and, especially, feelings of animosity. Until a time in which our communication has improved, it would be wise if we avoid asking too many questions targeted to personal areas of life. A good rule of thumb would be, "If they have not voluntarily shared, don't ask." We should always "test the waters" by asking non-intrusive questions. We should be sensitive and considerate of the other person's feelings when asking questions or sharing information. This will help us build our communication to a comfortable level of relating so that both parties become at ease with one another. This also helps build a foundation for development in our relationships.

Hollie's mother and I have a much different relationship than Shayna's mother and me. I believe that this stems from the differences in our personalities, how we relate to one another and, of course, our feelings toward one another. In addition, our awareness and consideration of the other person's feelings plays a key role in what we say, and how we say it.

How information is delivered goes from everyday "chit-chat" to in-depth conversations. The difference in what is discussed now, as compared to the past, is how comfortable we are with each other. This is because our feelings have changed over time. A good example is the day I called Hollie and her mother answered the phone. The third sentence that came out of her mouth was, "I am pregnant." If I still loved her, the way I once had, this would have hurt me deeply. If this had been several years ago, when I still had deep feelings for her and lacked skills to communicate artfully, this information blurted out would have caused me to have ill feelings and I would have negatively communicated my feelings. However, years had passed that created distance in my feelings for her so that her statement was just a statement delivering information.

Coincidentally, shortly after receiving that call, I received a call from Shayna's mother. She told me that she had a couple of things she needed to tell me. Although we had established an improved and positive form of communication, I still experienced a certain degree of hesitancy when I heard those words, because I had a much deeper emotional connection to her. She told me that she and Shayna would be out of town for a few weeks and would appreciate it if I would spend additional time with Shayna before their departure. Whew! Was that all? Not quite. She told me that there was something else she really needed to let me know, and before she could say it, I said, "You're pregnant." Baffled, she asked, "How did you know?" That was easy. I prepared myself knowing that this day would come, and my intuition had told me, two months previously, she would be pregnant within a few months. However, the point of this story is to illustrate that this was her way of respecting me by sharing a very intimate part of her personal life through artful expression. My personal feelings, and her personal life, were shared in a manner that nurtured our hearts, and expanded our spirits, because we respected areas in each other's lives that were off limits.

When communicating with our former spouse, topics such as our personal life should be off limits, unless our relationship has blossomed into a new friendship based on respect and unconditional love by both parties. Even then, there should be boundaries that should be set and respected. Change does not happen overnight. It takes time, patience, perseverance and, most of all, the desire to want a better and healthier relationship.

So, how do we know what we should consider to be subjects that are off limits? Think about meeting someone for the first time. What are some of the personal questions we ask? Do we ask anything personal? Not usually because we lack a close relationship and, more than likely, will not ask intrusive questions. We would not be sure of how our questions would be received and how that person may respond, so we tend to be more considerate and respectful. If we magnify this consideration and respect tenfold, we now have a measure of what we should or should not ask, or might share before we open our mouths while conversing with our former spouse. We should consider giving our former spouse the same consideration and respect we have for others.

It does not matter that once upon a time we had an intimate relationship with our former loved one and unveiled our heart's deepest secrets to this person. We should work on re-establishing trust through respect for our former spouse's personal life as we would in any new relationship. In time, together, we will determine the level at which it is appropriate for us to participate in each

## Communicating with a Former Spouse

other's lives. It is their decision, just as it is ours, to establish our boundaries. As it is for anyone else that we may come in contact, violating his or her boundaries not only becomes a felony in our relationship, it can impede future communication from growing at a rate deserved by both of us. If we find ourselves to have crossed over the set boundaries, we should be gentle on ourselves; after all we are only human. Our former spouse may respond unconsciously by attacking us or expressing their displeasure firmly. There is nothing wrong with their reaction. We should be aware of the fact that what we did was intrusive, acknowledge it, learn from it, and move on. We can rebound from our errors. We need to allow ourselves time to learn. We need to acknowledge that it takes time to establish a new relationship with our former spouse at whatever level is appropriate for the both of us. Most importantly, we should always remember that our motivating force is for the sake and well being of our children.

A relationship with anyone becomes personal when they allow us to share in the personal areas of their life. When they share personal information we are entrusted with their faith. These areas should not be abused or violated in any way to include negative criticism and judgment. Privacy, having a personal life, allows a former spouse separateness and freedom from the old roles we had in our marriage. This is important for all of us to understand. It allows us to re-establish our individuality and this helps us in the healing process from such feelings as victimization or guilt.

Maintaining a personal life separate from our former spouse is something most people yearn. There are also those people who will always gravitate back to their former spouse. This behavior comes from a lack of independence. Establishing our own life, separate from our former spouse, would not be difficult if we felt okay with ourselves. We all know that some people find security through another person. This often occurs in marriages in which some individuals traveled straight from the homes of their parents, into a marriage, and never really developed a life of their own. Thus, they only know how to be taken care of, instead of knowing how to take care of themselves, and to take responsibility for their lives. If this rings true for us, how can we develop our own personal life when we have been dependent on others, for most, or, for all of our lives? This dependence is the source of a need to remain a part of a former spouse's life.

Whatever reasons we may have to tell our former spouse about our own new life, or want to know what is happening in their life, we should resist the impulse. We should work at keeping our conversation civil and amicable, but somewhat detached, until we have built our communication to a point at which we can ask or share some small bit of personal news that is not construed as vindictive, or hurtful. We need to proceed with care and be very sensitive to the reactions of our former spouse. Trust and respect are something earned. They need to be re-established and built upon, particularly, if in the past, one or both of us has lacked sensitivity in this area. Key words to remember are trust, respect, consideration, and sensitivity. These coupled with unconditional love will guide us in knowing when and how much information we need to share.

## The Buckets

THE BUCKETS reprinted by permission of United Feature Syndicate, Inc.

# VI

## "What Works and What Doesn't?"

Many times I found myself preoccupied with trying to figure out what actually might work when I communicated with my former spouses. Instead of focusing on one specific area, my thoughts were often scattered. I learned to focus on one thought, idea, or issue at a time, which helped me feel less overwhelmed.

I remember feeling frustrated because I was trying so hard to improve the way in which I expressed myself, and yet I was not receiving the positive results I desired. This often led me to another desire: the desire to give up. Like many of my peers, I began to think that avoiding any communication with my former spouses sounded like the best remedy. Of course, I was left feeling hopeless which did not make me feel good at all. I wanted new tools, specific keys that would open any door of artful communication and allow consistent and positive results to show up in my life.

Having many friends who have divorced, you would think I would have learned "what works and what doesn't." Unfortunately, for the most part, it was my experience to become engulfed in other people's tragedies, rather than learning from their experiences. Like a bad daytime drama on television, we can be sucked into a variety of negative aspects in one episode and, gradually, come to the point where we expect the next episode to be even more twisted and tangled.

More and more people in our society seem to be preoccupied on focusing on the negative. Whatever happened to accentuating the positive, or visualizing the best outcome possible? So much of our time and energy is placed upon what we do not want to happen and we somehow seem to manifest our undesired result. Our energy should focus on the positive and desired results we want in our lives. Applying what others have learned is a good basis to begin improving our communication and is one way that can help us avoid potential problems.

Discovering "what works and what doesn't" can be a painstaking experience. Positive results can only occur if we acquire, learn, and practice new skills. There are many roads that may be traveled to reach the same destination. Each of us has to find the road that is best for us personally. Using the maps provided by the experiences of others is extremely helpful. However, in the end, which path to choose is something each of us needs to determine individually.

To assist us in this area, and with the help of others, I have collected some of the maps and road signs that can give us our positive and desired results. Sharing these experiences can benefit everyone. Of course, some of us may have already journeyed down roads using other maps that provided us with the positive results we were seeking, and I ask that you, in turn, share your wisdom with others when the opportunity arises. This is, at best, an incomplete list of keys, but it is a powerful list.

In a very real sense, "what works and what doesn't" is a compilation of gifts; each one provides positive results in some area of communication. Changing our current behavior and using one or more of these tools will help enrich our lives. The most important choice that needs to be made when selecting one or more of these tools to work with, is whether or not we want to keep our "need to be right." If we are willing to give up that need, these tools ARE effective.

## *What works (WW) and What Doesn't (WD):*

WW: Calling to say you are running late

WD: Showing up late with a perfunctory "Sorry" and it's not the first time

WW: Accepting that a difference of opinion exists

WD: We think the other person is wrong and, of course, we are right

WW: Knowing that we made a commitment for financial support and honoring that commitment

WD: Withholding financial support out of spite

WW: Accepting the realization that no harm was intended

WD: Wanting and seeking revenge

WW: Seeking counseling to work through any trauma we experienced

WD: Withdrawing from the world

## Communicating with a Former Spouse

WW: Turning to our higher power for comfort and guidance

WD: Turning to drugs, alcohol, and superficial relationships to forget what happened

WW: Artful communication (communication from our hearts)

WD: Forgetting that anyone has a heart

WW: Making positive changes in how we communicate

WD: Trying to change our former spouse

WW: Wanting to change in order to have better relationships

WD: Changing because someone else wants us to

WW: Listening
WD: Talking

WW: Starting communication with "I"
WD: Starting communication with "You"

WW: Agreeing not to discuss each other's present relationships

WD: Sharing with our former spouse how wonderful our new relationship is


WW: Building a new rapport

WD: Basing our communication on what happened in the past


WW: Focusing on the present

WD: Focusing on past issues and relationships


WW: Accepting the fact that our decision to end our relationship was not necessarily the right thing to do, and the willingness to make amends for any hurt we inflicted upon the other person

WD: Allowing pride to stand in the way of making amends, and not ever achieving any harmony


WW: Feeling good about ourselves

WD: Feeling like we are a failure

―――― *Communicating with a Former Spouse* ――――

WW: Accepting the fact that change is constant
WD: Resisting change

WW: Seeking counseling from a professional
WD: Seeking opinions from those who have gone through counseling and not experienced positive results

WW: Sticking to "what works" and building from there
WD: Repeating "what doesn't work" in hopes it will work some day

WW: Forgiving ourselves
WD: Forgiving everyone else but ourselves, or not forgiving anyone, including ourselves

WW: Remembering that outside influences affect our communication
WD: Allowing outside influences to affect our communication negatively (Example: a bad day at work)

WW: Keeping an open mind when listening to our former spouse's feelings and opinions

WD: Making them feel wrong for feeling and thinking the way they do

WW: Understanding that our former spouse is on the other side of the situation and our perspective is different

WD: Thinking that they see through our eyes and see the same picture

WW: Making a list of all the qualities we want our former spouse to exhibit when communicating with us, and we, by example, exhibit those qualities in our communication with them

WD: Waiting for our former spouse to exhibit these qualities before we do

WW: Visualizing the way we want our future communication to be like

WD: Thinking about how lousy our communication has been in the past

WW: Letting go of fear and embracing success

WD: Living in fear

WW: Being kind to ourselves
WD: Beating ourselves up

WW: Living without judgment (WARNING: This takes a lot of practice)
WD: Being judge, jury, and executioner!

WW: Giving ourselves permission to be vulnerable
WD: Not knowing the difference between being vulnerable and playing "victim"

WW: Living by example
WD: Talking about the way the other person should behave

WW: Proceeding with caution and awareness
WD: Ignoring possible warning signs

WW: Building and applying new and positive skills to communicate
WD: Relying solely on old skills for change

WW: Accepting that change is the only constant in the Universe

WD: Expecting people and situations to remain the same


WW: Filling our life with productive activities

WD: Remaining stagnant or participating in activities which are not in our best interest


WW: Setting boundaries around our personal life and surrounding ourselves with supportive individuals

WD: Not setting boundaries and allowing ourselves to be subjected to people or events that may be harmful to our well being


WW: Replacing old nonproductive habits with new ones

WD: Not filling the void of nonproductive habits, and being susceptible to them returning


WW: Taking inventory of our blessings

WD: Focusing on what we do not have

## Communicating with a Former Spouse

WW: Remembering that material things can be replaced

WD: Placing energy and emphasis on the material things we have lost


WW: Remembering that another person, place, or thing is not responsible for making us happy

WD: Relying on a person, place, or thing for our happiness


WW: Calling a friend when we are stuck, just to have someone listen to us

WD: Trying to rely solely on ourselves for comfort


WW: Speaking from our heart while expressing ourselves

WD: Allowing our head to control a conversation


WW: Offering a hand of friendship to our former spouse's new spouse

WD: Offering a finger (I think you can figure this one out)

WW: Doing something for someone else
WD: Focusing on our problems

WW: Making a list of the things we enjoy doing and doing one a week
WD: Not making time for ourselves and the things we enjoy

WW: Using the term "former" when referring to our former loved one and their family members
WD: Using "ex" (as in "x"... negated, negative, nothing—x'd out) to refer to these people

WW: Knowing that it is OK that family members do not understand how we feel
WD: Having to be understood before we can move on or feel OK with ourselves

WW: Understanding that our former in-laws or friends may not be comfortable in our presence
WD: Reacting to their awkwardness by allowing this to effect our self-esteem

WW: Treating our former in-laws with the same respect that we did while we were married
WD: Treating our former in-laws like "the plague"

WW: Remembering to honor and respect our feelings by taking a step back if a given issue overwhelms us
WD: Acting or reacting in haste to resolve an issue

WW: Making a decision that is beneficial to everyone, even though it may not be a popular view
WD: Not making a decision because not everyone will be happy and we want everyone to like us

WW: Accepting support
WD: Rejecting support because we think we do not need others

WW: Giving first
WD: Waiting to receive before we give

WW: Enjoying the fact that we are still alive after our divorce

WD: Living in a self-made hell of regrets, anger, guilt, or whatever manifestation our private hell provides

Some of these contributions are standard artful communication skills applicable to many of life's situations. Others, are helpful hints specific to the situation of divorce. All of them, however, have proven of value to those who have used them.

## A NOTE ON AVOIDANCE

Something that sticks out when discussing a former spouse with others is the phenomenon of *avoidance.* Avoidance can emerge from things like arguments or differences of opinion. Hostility and frustration show up in conversations and rather than deal with differences, the tendency is to avoid future contact. Avoiding communicating with our former spouse seems to work as a solution because it creates a buffer zone, a time when there is no apparent conflict. Some individuals have reported that the way they communicate with their former spouse is simply not to!

In reality, most of us must communicate with our former spouses because of our children. But some people go long periods without speaking to their former spouse. They believe by not speaking to them they are not thinking about them. When speaking becomes unavoidable, hostility and frustration emerge, thereby, creating turmoil and upheavals in their lives, for days, even weeks (yes, they really were thinking about them, having internal dialogues and arguments). Learning to establish functional and artful communication on any level helps alleviate feelings of hostility and frustration. It may be that these feelings will never go away completely, but they can be reduced, and as a result, less time and energy is spent on negative feelings.

Avoidance is a trap. It gives a false feeling that everything is going well, when in fact nothing has changed; nothing can change without active participation. Like a drug, it gives a temporary feeling of relief, but when the moment for dealing with reality comes we do not function at our best. Avoidance is a quick fix for a situation that requires multi-level attention. Learning to take action to deal with situations will, over a period of time, create change. Quality communication with a former spouse is not something that occurs overnight. It is not something that happens as a single event, or a magic moment. It is a high-maintenance activity, and avoiding communication, in most instances, make our situations more difficult.

Also, consider this: If parents do not take the opportunities they have to communicate with each other, what conclusions are children reaching? What lessons do they incorporate into their lives? Do they learn to run away from anything challenging? Do they learn to avoid involvement in relationships? Are they learning how to get along?

Avoidance is just one more action that does not work in divorce relationships when children are involved. We must face this reality in order to move forward when we look at "what works and what doesn't." When we are open to improving our communication, our feeling of avoiding communicating with our former loved one will lessen over time. Only then can we apply some of the things that have worked for others.

## CHILDREN

*The greatest reverence is due the young.*
—Juvenal

Since our goal is to create a positive environment for our children, and ourselves, a special section to address the issue of our children and our relationship with them has been created. Many of these "what works and what doesn't" statements apply whether a family is divorced or intact, but they take on special importance for the vulnerable children of a divorced family. Even though many partners in a divorce feel victimized by their situation, it is the children who are the *real* victims, and sometimes we overlook this reality with all that goes on in our lives. If we take the following thoughts to heart, we give a wonderful gift to our children.

WW: Remembering children are a part of both parents
WD: Conveniently forgetting the other parent is still alive

WW: Discussing consistency in raising children
WD: Having different values in different homes

WW: Speaking to children together on important issues
WD: Assuming they do not need an explanation

WW: Making it very clear to our children that the divorce is in no way their fault
WD: Avoiding conversations with our children regarding the divorce

WW: Keeping children out of our differences with our former spouse
WD: Using our children as weapons

WW: Encouraging our children to call their non-custodial parent

WD: Assuming that since they show no desire to call the other parent, there is no benefit or reason for them to do so

WW: Making sure our children send cards to our former spouse on Christmas, Birthdays, or "just because" letters, pictures, report cards, etc.

WD: Thinking none of this matters to our former spouse because he or she never asks

WW: Encouraging our former spouse to take our children on trips or just overnight

WD: Hoping our former spouse will never ask to spend more time with them

WW: Participating in our children's school activities and being a part of their world

WD: Spending most of the time with our children in an adult world

WW: Being a friend to our children *and* a parent
WD: Being only a parent

## Communicating with a Former Spouse

WW: Frequently telling our children we love them
WD: Forgetting that our children need emotional nurturing and reinforcement

WW: Telling our children about our former spouse's good qualities
WD: Saying anything but nice things about our former spouse

WW: Never forgetting our children's birthdays or other special occasions
WD: Expecting our children to understand why we forgot a special day

WW: Playing silly games with our children
WD: Telling our children that what they are doing is childish

WW: Allowing our children to be children
WD: Expecting our children to act as adults

WW: Honoring our children because they are the hope of the future
WD: Seeing our children as not having the ability or opportunity to live their dreams

WW: Spending quality (and quantity) time with our children, whether we are the custodial parent or not... anyone can be a baby-sitter... we are parents

WD: Parking our children in front of the TV because we have too much to do right now

WW: Finding out where our children need the most help in their education and providing that extra support

WD: Not taking a personal interest and involvement in our children's education

WW: Learning to accept that a stepparent may appear on the scene or is already there, and knowing that our bond with our children can never, never, be broken

WD: Competing with a stepparent

WW: Assisting in building our children's self-esteem by encouraging them to investigate their interests

WD: Suppressing our children's interests because of our own desires for their future

WW: When our children do something wrong, before we respond, thinking about the things we did at their age (our own parents can be very helpful in pointing these things out)

WD: Basing our response on adult experience and forgetting our children's age

WW: Using positive words to investigate an issue with our children

WD: Verbally abusing our children to impose our solution of an issue upon them

WW: Letting go of the negative things that may have been said by our children's grandparents

WD: Holding on to negative feelings we have toward our children's grandparents that can be detected by our children

## NOW IT IS YOUR TURN...

While it is impractical to expect everyone to obtain the same results, the goal is for us to find value in these lists. As you use one, some, or all of these tools, you should be aware of what other things have worked and not worked for you. I fully realize that the lists are incomplete. One person cannot visualize all the possible situations and challenges for everyone who goes through a divorce. I invite you to sit down and write a list of, "what works and what doesn't work" for you and to keep a running log in the future. You may constantly refer back to it until you have committed it to memory, and have practiced it enough for it to become a new set of behaviors.

If you have a "what works" that is not on the list, you should write it down and acknowledge yourself for having found a means of dealing with another situation. If you note down something that has NOT worked for you, and do not have a "what works" to offset it, writing it down may trigger some other possible solution for you. You should acknowledge yourself for at least recognizing that you have discovered a challenge that you want to address.

WW: _____
WD: _____

WW: _____
WD: _____

WW: _____
WD: _____

## Communicating with a Former Spouse

WW: _____
WD: _____

WW: _____
WD: _____

WW: _____
WD: _____

WW: _____
WD: _____

WW: _____
WD: _____

WW: _____
WD: _____

WW: _____
WD: _____

WW: _____
WD: _____

———— *Vincent Gerard Molina* ————

WW: _____
WD: _____

WW: _____
WD: _____

WW: _____
WD: _____

WW: _____
WD: _____

WW: _____
WD: _____

WW: _____
WD: _____

WW: _____
WD: _____

WW: _____
WD: _____

*———— Communicating with a Former Spouse ————*

WW: _____
WD: _____


WW: _____
WD: _____


WW: _____
WD: _____


WW: _____
WD: _____


WW: _____
WD: _____


WW: _____
WD: _____


WW: _____
WD: _____


WW: _____
WD: _____

*Vincent Gerard Molina*

WW: _____
WD: _____

WW: _____
WD: _____

WW: _____
WD: _____

WW: _____
WD: _____

WW: _____
WD: _____

WW: _____
WD: _____

WW: _____
WD: _____

WW: _____
WD: _____

## Communicating with a Former Spouse

WW: _____
WD: _____

WW: _____
WD: _____

WW: _____
WD: _____

WW: _____
WD: _____

WW: _____
WD: _____

WW: _____
WD: _____

WW: _____
WD: _____

WW: _____
WD: _____

# HAPPINESS:

*The quality or state of being happy.*

# VII

## Happily Ever After: Can It Happen?

    Fairy tales are wonderful stories that are told to us when we are children, but as we grow older, many of us who try to live these fairy tales become disillusioned with life. Fairy tales are only meant to entertain us. Many people have a set idea programmed in their minds before getting married, "He is the 'prince' or 'knight in shining armor,' she is the 'damsel waiting to be swept off her feet and rescued,' like 'Sleeping Beauty' or 'Snow White.'" The fact is that many of us are blinded to the reality that marriage takes effort by both husband and wife, every single day. A marriage is not something that runs on automatic pilot. This is when reality slaps us in the face. But we can live happily ever after if we choose to make the commitment and honest effort to work on our marriages. Yes, as stated previously, we have a choice and the choice is up to us. Whether married, or divorced, we choose how we feel, happy or not. It is not our work, family, friends, spouse, or any other person, place, or thing that decides our happiness. By now, we should all realize that our happiness has nothing to do with our former spouse. This one small but significant fact should empower us to apply new methods that will enhance our level of communication we currently have with our former mate.

Although it is my hope that *Communicating with a Former Spouse* will help millions of people, there will always be those who may never improve the relationship they have now with their former spouse. This is a reality of life because some of us choose not to put forth the effort required to change our current situations. Not changing may stem from fear, low self-esteem, laziness, who knows? The information in this book is provided to provoke new thought, new awareness, or to stir old thought for those of us who have a desire to improve our lives. Desire is not enough; a person must take action.

We do not have to know where our former spouse lives to create greater relationships and have a happier life. Just having the ability to switch our way of thinking, or thought process concerning our former spouse can help to create a better life for our children and us. If our former spouse is missing, we may never know when our former spouse will walk back into our children's life and, therefore, into our own. Communicating with a former spouse goes beyond verbal skills; it is also what we project outward as a result of what we feel inside. We can create positive thoughts, unconditional love, and above all, forgive our former spouse, and ourselves, or whatever applies to our individual situation.

The ability to love and be loved is learned behavior. Love gives us power beyond material things. Only we can fill our lives with love. As individuals, we hold more power than any nation. We can destroy ourselves in a split second, or we can create for ourselves an abundance of love. By creating love and artfully communicating, love emerges in a variety of ways. It begins with a willingness to love ourselves first and the desire to create harmonious relationships with others.

Life is not a fairy tale; thus, perfect relationships do not exist. However, we can create positive results in our relationships that will, ultimately, grant us a better life. If life were a fairy tale, challenges would not exist because our results would always be the same: perfect. We cannot grow without challenges. Good, bad, or indifferent, the events that take place in our lives allow us to experience many feelings, emotions and thoughts. What is important is how we choose to act, or react, to our experiences.

## CHOICES IN LIFE

We are blessed with the opportunity to make our own choices in life. As stated throughout this text, there is no person, place, or thing that exists that can control the way we feel. Although, other people do not control the way we feel, much of their words and actions may be in conflict with our own beliefs. When someone says or does something that goes against our belief system, we may feel hurt, angry, disappointment, resentment, or vengeful. It is our thoughts that create the feelings we experience and the way we react to any given situation.

Some people may disagree with the previous statement and feel frustrated. What a person reads does not make them feel frustrated. It is our choice of reaction that generates a specific emotion. It is in this way that we tend to give up our control to others. We need to take charge of our emotional reactions and take control over our lives in order to change. Letting go of our former spouse, and getting on with our own lives, helps us to develop positive communication with our former loved ones and others. Sometimes letting go is a painstaking process because of our need to hold on to a "thing." Feeling uncomfortable about direct contact with our former spouse is a normal feeling. Even the anticipation of contact with them causes many of us anxiety. Proceeding in this manner generates negative nonverbal communication when contact does occur. Usually, our feelings, no matter how we may try to hide them, do not go undetected. It is our body language, avoidance of eye contact, and tone of voice that conveys tension. These create unfavorable reactions from our former spouse. Once we learn to let go, becoming more relaxed is inevitable. This creates calmer conversations and our way of relating is enhanced.

For most couples, communication does not improve on its own after divorce, although it may seem that way at first. Communicating may appear to improve due to the superficial nature of the conversation that occurs. We may have discussed what happened, what went wrong for us, and perhaps, went to family counseling. But after that, for many of us, not much else happens, or is accomplished, once a husband and wife have legally parted ways. If we are honest, we do not always want to get to the bottom of things, and some of us have difficulty moving on to "life after divorce."

Although many of us would like to think we have improved communication after divorce, it may actually get worse by creating a significant distance or by "hiding out." When we do have conversations with our former spouse, they may sound like this: "Hi, how is work and how are the kids? I thought I would call to see how the kids are doing." Most of us are experts in safe, polite, and non-threatening conversation.

Do we really, and I mean *really*, share our true thoughts and feelings after divorce? If we appear to have a harmonious relationship, it may be due to the fact that we choose to avoid in-depth topics and real feelings. Some divorced couples do not seem to get past a few sentences without raising their voices, accusing, attacking, defending, picking, lecturing, or heavy sighing. For these couples, avoiding real feelings is the chosen and preferable way of communicating.

Not every relationship with a former spouse will encompass in-depth topics, like every day challenges of life, or current world events. However, when we sincerely express our real feelings around issues that effect our relationship, this allows us to respect ourselves and maintain our dignity. If we avoid important issues that affect our relationship, we may invite a variety of negative feelings that will fracture our connection.

How should we communicate with our former spouse? If superficial conversation keeps peace, should we stick to it? At what point in a relationship do two people consciously or unconsciously decide to communicate like they barely know one another; as if they never experienced that person as more than just an acquaintance? Did we ever really know this person? Who is this person and why do we want to communicate with them? These notions remind me of a giant vacuum that has sucked all the caring and spirituality we once shared with our former loved ones right out of our brains and we become numb. Like robots or monotone voices that express non-existent emotion, a sort of semi-lobotomy that still allows us to speak but lacks all human feeling.

No one ever told us that life after divorce would be challenging, and for some of us, more challenging than marriage. I am, of course, referring to the area of communication. A common misconception is that little contact and little communication equals fewer problems.

*Misconception: little contact + little communication = fewer problems.*

Avoidance does not relieve or solve any problem. If anything, it adds to the dread we feel when we know we must speak with our former spouse. Ideally, we should work on these areas, but in reality many of us do not.

Not to worry, we only have to work on ourselves to improve communication with others. Who said you must like someone to communicate with them? We only need to come from a space of love and caring to communicate artfully and authentically.

## DESIRE AND . . .

There is no fast path or guaranteed solution to improved communication with a former spouse. Many of us say we would like better communication, and many of us say we have tried, but to no avail did many of us succeed. My question is, "How strong is our desire and what are we willing to do to improve upon our communication with our former spouse?"

As with many things we want out of life, all it takes is a strong enough desire, commitment, and action to obtain our desired results. There is just one more thing that we must do to make this work; *get out of our own way.* We have a tendency to see our obstacle as our former spouse, when in reality, we may be the obstacle to fulfilling our desires.

How willing are we to create an artful level of communication that allows us to function in a way that is mutually beneficial for everyone? I am not talking about living in perfect balance of each other's expectations. I am talking about having enough mutual respect to establish a common ground that operates in an environment of non-judgment.

I am not a rocket scientist, the Dali Lama, or a prophet, but I do know that the universal law of give and

## Communicating with a Former Spouse

receive apply just as much to a relationship with our former spouse as it does with everyone else in our lives. The power of our heart is so vital to all of our relationships, once our heart is broken the effects can be devastating and long lasting.

Effectively communicating with a former spouse is a journey, not a destination. It can be a very unpleasant journey, or one that we barely notice. There will always be detours, bumps, and areas that need maintenance and repairs. Then again, all relationships in our lives are the same in this respect. The road that I personally traveled, prior to making changes in my life, was not a road at all. It was one of the biggest, scariest, longest roller coasters I had ever ridden. At times, I felt I was making ground going uphill. Just when it felt really good to be on top with a clear view of everything around me, I fell. I also tumbled through a few loops. As the ride started to level off, and speed increased, it felt like I had swirled through a couple of corkscrews.

Some of us find an amusement park roller coaster exciting enough to go back on, over and over again. The emotional trauma of this metaphorical ride was so unbearable that I could not wait to get off. There was only one way for me to get off and stay off that wild ride. I decided to change my life by improving my self-expression.

What I find intriguing is that, generally, we see our former spouse with all the frustration, anger, and hurt we can muster up in an emotional picture. These pictures may be easily created because of the intense love we once shared, and for some, still feel. The more people I meet, the more there are those who say that they lack the knowledge and skills to communicate effectively because they do not know how to cope with some of their negative emotions. Those people who learned to communicate effectively and artfully shared that change was possible after years of suffering. Who made them change? They did. Why? They got tired of their own negative feelings and self-defeating emotions. They wanted a happier life.

There does not seem to be a day that goes by where I do not meet someone who has either been divorced or is in a relationship with a former spouse where children are involved. Some of these individuals have expressed to me a broad range of revelations. One that specifically stands out is that someone told me that their choice to have a child was not well thought out or even planned. This person said they married too quickly before discovering what was important to them and to their loved one. They married without taking into consideration the impact the other person would have on their life when they committed to a life-long partnership. They said they did not realize the level of commitment marriage required and were not ready to put forth the effort their partnership needed to flourish.

*Misconception: Neither marriage nor a former spouse relationship requires much maintenance.*

Paying too little attention to either one of these relationships causes increasing decay and can lead to a multitude of problems that requires more energy than most of us care to expend. It is amazing to me how many people view marriage as something so disposable. So many people get married without really knowing the other person, to say nothing of knowing themselves. I advocate self-development workshops and seminars that would be offered to couples before they marry. Courses like, "Who am I?" or "How to Love Me First" and, "How to Become Independent and Stay that Way," would be abundantly practical. These curriculums would target self-awareness and discovery. This would not necessarily prevent divorce; however, this conscious awareness could impact whether individuals married sooner than they were ready. I would also recommend couples to participate in *Intellectual Foreplay*, a wonderfully insightful book, by Eve Hogan. This book contains questions for couples who want to learn more about each other, and themselves.

There are numerous lessons to be learned about who we are and what motivates us, whether we are married or divorced. If we are conscious enough to see value in these lessons, we will learn from them. Learning "what works and what doesn't work" in our lives, acquiring and practicing new skills, and creating a new relationship with ourselves will assist us in making sound choices. This is possible because we have gained knowledge that helps us to reach new levels of self-development and growth. At the bare minimum, we will have a newly found conscious awareness in the areas where we once needed assistance in order for us to make better decisions.

If we are blinded to the gifts of a challenging situation or circumstance, we tend to give up because we are unable to see that hope exists. If hope is visible we may still choose to give up because we may be unwilling to put forth any effort required for change to take place. Our situations can change if we give serious thought to the possible ramifications that our lack of action will have on our children, and ourselves, over a long period of time. There may be several reasons for us to want to establish functional, effective, authentic, and artful communication with our former spouse. But there is only one very important reason and motivation for us to do so. *Our children deserve to have a better life.*

If we have not figured it out yet, an extremely large portion of society has been married at least once before. If we take a look around, a really good look, we see that a large percentage of our nation's adult population is divorced. Observe the people around us. There must be dozens, if not hundreds, or maybe thousands we pass by every day. Some of us may currently be in a new relationship, while others are still recuperating from their divorce. Wherever we fit, chances are that our current or next relationship will be with someone who is divorced. If we ponder this, then we understand that they too are a former spouse and may experience what we experience as a former spouse, or they experience the same thing as our former spouse. This is a sobering thought, is it not? There is no good or bad here, it is only to point out that the majority of former spouses have issues with their situations. What we tend to overlook is the simple fact that our former spouse is just like us, they too want peace of mind, happiness, hope, and love. It takes but one of us to start the process of getting along harmoniously and laying the groundwork for such a relationship to occur.

## Vincent Gerard Molina

### Non Sequitur

© 1995, The Washington Post. Reprinted with permission.

## NEW RELATIONSHIPS

*A journey of a thousand miles must begin with a single step.*

—Lao-Tzu

When we choose to enter into a new relationship, do we really give any thought to how our relationship with our former spouse may influence our relationship with another individual? If this new person has a former spouse, do we give thought to how their relationship with their former loved one will influence our relationship? How would it feel to be involved in a new relationship and our present love is a parent, but has unresolved feelings and lacks communication with their former spouse? Does this impact us positively, or negatively? Healthy communication with a former spouse can only enhance another relationship. Some couples have expressed that they do not appreciate their current mate's relationship with their former spouse. They have expressed feelings of jealousy and resentment. While it is true that an individual can carry a relationship with a former spouse to an extreme, most people experience insecurity because they are threatened by the intimacy their new love once shared with another person. Communicating with a former spouse is not intimacy; it is something that is established to bring greater peace to our lives and to the lives of our children. Even though a person's intention may be to create a stress-free relationship with their former spouse solely for the benefit and well being of their children, a current spouse or partner may interpret this relationship as threatening to their current love relationship. It is only through our consideration of these feelings that they will be able to understand that a harmonious relationship with our former spouse also augments harmony in our relationship with them.

As we establish positive and healthier communication with our former spouse, we become an example for others with whom we come in contact. Our win is their win. By example, we provide hope, encouragement, and inspiration for others to take action in their lives. People will want what we have acquired; more peace of mind.

Whether married or divorced, communication is a vital key to success in all relationships, in the workplace, and at home. We need to understand that it can be just as difficult to communicate to our partner in a new marriage as with a former spouse. If we lack the desire to achieve harmony and we do not nurture our relationships they will not grow. It is that simple. All relationships require conscious awareness. All relationships require constant effort. Relationships cannot survive without nurturing.

## THE REAL VICTIMS

The real victims of poor communication between former spouses are not the spouses themselves. The real victims are our children. When we choose not to communicate on a level that is mutually beneficial with our former loved one we send negative messages to our children. If children experience a disharmonious environment because of a less than harmonious relationship between their parents, how do we think they feel? When a parent uses negative language toward their former spouse, how do children view that other parent? For that matter, how do children view the parent who makes the negative comments? Children receive mixed messages because their experience with a particular parent may be a positive one, and not the negative experience that one parent voices about the other. Is Mommy bad? Is Daddy bad? What are our children to think? Do we think that they may feel our divorce was their fault? Do they think the reason their parents cannot, or do not communicate is because of something they did or did not do? Bet on it. Sometimes, children blame themselves for their parents divorce because they want to believe that their parents can do no wrong.

Parents do not have to hide the fact from their children that they do not agree with one another. They only have to demonstrate that they can have healthy communication with each other for the well being of their children. The example we set for our children will affect how they feel about us, and most importantly, about themselves.

Remember that our children did not have a choice in whether or not we divorced. We did not ask them, "What do you think, should mommy and daddy divorce?" They were, and remain, spectators. All they know is that the two most important people in their life made the decision to break up their family unit. All they know is that they come home to only one parent daily. This is a cold hard fact. Why would we want to contribute any more to their hardship? It would better serve our children if we learned to establish healthy communication with our former spouse where everyone is satisfied. There are instances where this is absolutely not possible, but they are few. Most cases simply require our willingness to take action.

Once again, *happiness can only be found within ourselves.* If we are to live happily ever after, then we must experience inner happiness first. Inner happiness comes from loving ourselves and being happy with who we are and what we have, not who we want to be and what we do not have. As we learn to love and accept ourselves for who we are, we create a vacuum that will attract the things we desire. Said another way; we are like a magnet that attracts those things we desire most in life. Our vision becomes clearer. The messages we send out subconsciously are received by those people and things we would like to have in our lives. Our messages call upon these desires to enter our lives. Learning to find joy in life is just a thought away.

Joy lies in the spirit of what we do, as well as, how we do it. We can experience joy in eating a hamburger, as well as, communicating with our former spouse. Joy is *not* the hamburger; *it is in the act of eating the hamburger*. Joy is *not* communicating with our former spouse; *it is the spirit in which we communicate*. Joy is not enough; we must also become passionate.

Having a passion for life can only be seen through the eyes of a person who is not blinded by hate, resentment, and victimization. The world is a playground meant to be enjoyed and embraced. There is opportunity to receive as much as we want, providing we are open to receiving it. In order to have the things we want most in life, we need to embrace life by feeling and demonstrating passion in everything we do. Everyone is capable of experiencing and feeling passion. Passion is demonstrated as we embrace every moment in our day, taking time out to count our blessings and displaying our greatness by using our natural abilities and sharing our talents with others.

Our natural abilities and talents were not given to us solely for our own use and benefit. Life is made up of pieces of a puzzle, each of us represents one piece. When we are placed together, we share these pieces and everyone prospers. Each of us is unique. Each of us has a gift that only we possess. When we share our gift with others, we share pieces of ourselves and, as it was meant to be, we make connections with other spiritual beings. These pieces that define us also make us unique. They are particles of our spirit. I believe that our spirit is the source from which our passion comes from. It is our spirit that allows us to love, be loved, and forgive. What we have experienced through the hardship of divorce can either make us stronger or, if we allow it to, can damage our spirit, irreparably. The choice of how we feel and how we react is always up to us.

Life provides all sorts of opportunities and challenges. If we believe in God, we know that God only gives us things we can handle. It then becomes our choice whether or not we exercise our free agency; the right to choose to become wiser, stronger, and embrace life, or reject opportunity and challenge because of the actions of another spiritual being.

Our inability to see that life has something to offer stops us from obtaining what we desire most in life. The most difficult challenge, one that is common when communicating with a former spouse, is our reluctance to work at changing our situation. Life provides us the means to acquire happiness and greater relationships, but there will always be some of us who will not make the choice to have either. Instead their choice is to refuse and not to reach out and grasp their opportunities. We can expend energy into why our life does not work, how we were wronged, who is to blame, and never put energy into creating a new life for us.

## ABUNDANCE

Abundance can be defined as having a surplus, simply having more than enough or having an excess. Each individual according to their perceptions of life can define living abundantly. Abundance may come in the form of money, possessions, love, spirituality, and relationships. For the sake of the topic at hand, living in abundance can be viewed as an abundance of healthy relationships, including one with our former spouse. To attain healthy relationships with others, we must first have a healthy relationship with ourselves. Even then, there will be people in our lives who will not allow us to, or want to engage in healthy communication and relationships with us, but the key exists in our own attitudes and reactions. Remember, we choose how we feel about the way others act towards us.

To create an abundance of love, we first accept ourselves unconditionally; no matter what choices we made in the past. The choice we make now is where our focus should be placed. Choosing to love ourselves is possible when we accept who we are, "warts and all."

*Vincent Gerard Molina*

Getting past our physical being is only difficult when we focus on our earthly human qualities and remain distant from the spiritual qualities we all possess. Spirit is our natural being. The earthly qualities we all have are bestowed to us at birth and are not a part of our spirit. For the most part, we allow our parents, teachers, friends and circumstances to affect how we feel about ourselves. We may have come from a broken home, had a substance abuse problem, or been told we were stupid. Maybe we were fired from a job, went to jail, were a prostitute, or maybe our spouse cheated on us and left us for another person. We can either let our past dictate our lives or we can realize that it has no place in the choices we make and who we are today. How we feel about ourselves today decides our truth, not what happened in our past and not what other people tell us. If we love ourselves abundantly, we will live in an abundance of love.

We need to respect ourselves. In other words, we do not violate ourselves by making choices that are harmful to us. When we are at a crossroads and need to make a choice, before deciding, we should ask ourselves, "Does this feel good?" Then, we need to listen to our hearts. We need to practice listening to our hearts. In the past, we have probably listened to our heads and thought that it was our heart talking. Our hearts are very wise. When we incorporate our heart with our head, we form a winning team that is able to make good sound choices.

As we improve, it becomes easier to make better choices because we automatically begin to use both of our great faculties. We need to make a conscious effort in using both heart and head when making choices. Practicing this skill daily will help us. Do we think that if we were more conscious of the decisions we make, and how we make them, that we would make better decisions? And, if we became consciously aware and stopped to ask our hearts, "Does this feel good?" we just might make better decisions in the future.

As we become more in touch with how our decisions affect us, we will gain more respect for ourselves. As we respect ourselves more, we will learn to respect others more. Said earlier, it is a natural by-product that how we feel about ourselves is how we communicate with others. If we love ourselves, we love others. If we are angry with ourselves, we are angry with others. If we do not have control over our lives, we have a need to control others. Greater relationships with others happen when we add the necessary element of self-respect into our lives to achieve a happier state of being.

*Vincent Gerard Molina*

## IT CAN HAPPEN

*We are the hero of our own story.*
—Mary McCarthy

As a result of my faith, hope in humanity, and a lot of effort, I believe I continue to create the best possible relationships I can develop with my former spouses. I know that we have daughters who feel loved by both of their parents, every day. Hollie is a teenager, and when asked to recall the last time her mother and I fought, she is unable to remember. She will, however, acknowledge that her mother and father disagree on many things. Best of all, she will tell anyone who listens that we both love her very much and I know this is due to our efforts at establishing healthy communication.

Shayna is currently in pre-school, and is also a child of a very healthy relationship between former spouses, even though we separated during her mother's pregnancy. Although Shayna and I have never lived in the same household together, it is very clear to her who I am in her life. There is no doubt in my mind that Shayna will always feel loved by both of us, as a direct result of the healthy communication we have been willing to establish and continue to nurture.

To get to this point in the lives of our daughters, the participants had to have the desire for a relationship that allowed us to respect each other, and ourselves. From mutual respect came the ability to communicate effectively, functionally, artfully, and authentically with one another. As with all parties to a relationship in life, we will never agree on everything. We will, however, continue to learn and practice the art of communicating in which one does not have to lose for the other one to win. This type of approach fosters support in our own lives, as well as setting an example for our daughters, and their future love relationships.

Children all over the world have the opportunity to experience this kind of love when their parents decide that they are willing to make the effort to give it to them. A child's environment has an impact on their behavior and attitudes. Parents are not able to be there every moment of the day with their children to make sure they are not victimized, or exposed to experiences that can be detrimental to their well being. Parents can, however, always provide guidance by being a good and positive example when they are with their children.

Nine times out of ten the phrase "you're just like your father," or "you're just like your mother," refers to a less-than-positive quality. I would like to leave this physical world knowing that when someone says to my children, "you're just like your father," they are referring to the qualities that have had a positive impact on their lives and my children will recognize this as a compliment.

The choice is ours to take what we know, learn more, and apply it to having healthy communication with our former spouse. The result will be a new relationship that will promote love and allow children to be more secure in that knowledge. By giving our children a solid emotional base and demonstrating for them the skills necessary for an authentic relationship, we give them the tools needed for the future. Every parent wishes that his or her children will experience an enduring relationship of their own someday and will be happier by virtue of the lessons taught them.

## YES, IT CAN HAPPEN!

## About the Author

Vincent Gerard Molina spent over 17 years in the corporate world. He discovered during that time that there was more to life than big business, the traditional forty-hour week and paycheck. He wanted to make a larger and profound impact on humanity.

Through his professional experience, personal development, and communication training, along with real life experiences, Vincent redefined his life. His mission is to improve human relationships and business skills through innovative methods. Vincent surrounds himself with some of the most successful mentors, advisors, and trainers who all share one thing: the knowledge of helping others.

Vincent grew up in Hawaii and now resides in Utah. He is a successful speaker, corporate trainer, researcher, and facilitator of workshops and seminars. He is the proud father of two wonderful girls and husband of a beautiful and supportive wife.

Vincent Gerard Molina is available for workshops, seminars, and lectures. If you are interested, please call:

1 (888) 474-2962

# Notes

# Notes